IN REMEMBRANCE OF ME

IN REMEMBRANCE
OF ME

by

ALEXANDER WHYTE

BAKER BOOK HOUSE
Grand Rapids, Michigan

Reprinted 1970 by
Baker Book House Company

Reprinted from the original
edition published in 1906 by
A. C. Armstrong and Son, New York

PHOTOLITHOPRINTED BY CUSHING - MALLOY, INC.
ANN ARBOR, MICHIGAN, UNITED STATES OF AMERICA
1 9 7 0

CONTENTS

1

THE COMFORTS OF GOD

"Comfort ye, comfort ye My people, saith your God."—
Isa. xl. 1.

" The boundless exhilaration " of Isaiah is a proverb in sacred letters. There is nothing, anywhere else in literature, sacred or profane, to compare with the hope, the joy, the rapture, the transport of Isaiah. The Book of Revelation itself— that so transcendent book—goes back, and borrows some of its most captivating visions, as well as some of its sublimest language, from the Book of Isaiah. The New Testament has so completely taken over into itself this Old Testament book, that it is impossible for us to read this book any more, simply as Isaiah wrote it.

When we read of Babylon in Isaiah, we immediately think of our own bondage to sin. When we read of Cyrus, we have already forgotten Cyrus, because we have seen Christ. When our students study " the Servant of the Lord " in Isaiah, their hearts turn to their Saviour, and they say to Him : " Lo, now speakest Thou plainly, adn speakest no

parable.   For Thou hast in very deed been
wounded for our transgressions, and bruised for
our iniquities, and the Lord hath laid on Thee
the iniquity of us all." And when we read in the
eloquent prophet how the wilderness was trans-
formed into the garden of the Lord around the
returning exiles, it is far more wonderful, and far
more eloquent to us,—the way the Lord is leading
ourselves. Nor can we read Isaiah's noble de-
scription of his and his people's New Jerusalem,
without our heart melting within us to be for ever
home in the Jerusalem which is above, which is
free, and which is the mother of us all.

No less than twenty-seven chapters of Isaiah's
great book are taken up with the comfort of the
captives in Babylon. And large and evangelical
as is the scope, rich and far-reaching as is the
vision, and surpassingly eloquent as is the style of
those twenty-seven chapters—at the same time
every word of those chapters is spoken and written
for the comfort of the captive people. And the
" incomparable exhilaration " of those twenty-
seven chapters is all due to this—that " the God of
all comfort " not only gives Isaiah his commission
of comfort, but puts the very comforts themselves,
as well as the very words in which those comforts
are to be described, into the prophet's mouth.
The God of Israel rises up to comfort His people
Himself in this golden book. Only, He conveys

those comforts through the golden heart and the golden mouth of this greatly-gifted and greatly-graced prophet. So much have we of God Himself in this book, and so little of Isaiah—beyond his name and his voice—that we may take this book as all but the speech and the penmanship of the Divine Comforter Himself, carrying out His own command : " Comfort ye, comfort ye My people. Speak ye comfortably to Jerusalem ; speak to her heart "

Supper being ended, when Jesus knew that His hour was come that He should depart out of this world to the Father, He set Himself to comfort His sorrowing disciples. When Simon Peter said to Him, " Lord, whither goest Thou ? " Jesus answered him : " Let not your heart be troubled : ye believe in God, believe also in Me. In My Father's house are many mansions : I go to prepare a place for you. And if I go and prepare a place for you, I will come again and receive you to Myself : that where I am, there ye may be also." And when Thomas raised this difficulty, " Lord, we know not whither Thou goest ; and how can we know the way ? " Jesus comforted Thomas with these great words : " I am the Way, the Truth, and the Life." And when Judas raised *his* difficulty, " Lord, how is it that Thou wilt manifest Thyself to us, and not to the world ? " his Master explained to him : " If a man love Me, he

will keep My words; and My Father will love
him, and We will come unto him and make Our
abode with him." And then, from that, our Lord
passed on to promise and to describe the Holy
Ghost as "Another Comforter," whom the Father
will send to them in answer to His prayer. And it
is of the first importance to every New Testament
disciple to have ever before him the very words
in which our Lord describes and promises the Holy
Ghost. "I will pray the Father, and He will give
you another Comforter, that He may abide with
you for ever. And ye know Him: for He
dwelleth with you, and shall be in you. The Father
will send the Comforter in My name, and He shall
teach you all things and bring all things to your
remembrance, whatsoever I have said to you. It
is expedient for you that I go away: for if I go not
away, the Comforter will not come unto you; but if
I depart, I will send Him to you. He shall guide
you into all truth. He shall take of Mine and shall
show it unto you. These things I have spoken
unto you, that in Me ye might have peace. In the
world ye shall have tribulation: but be of good
cheer; I have overcome the world."

1. Now, in passing on to apply all that to ourselves, the first thing is to raise the question
whether this comfort, or any part of it, belongs at
all to us. "Comfort ye, comfort ye *My people*,
saith your God." "The world cannot receive the

Comforter," says our Lord, "because it seeth Him not, neither knoweth Him." The Holy Ghost is sent to the world indeed,—but not as a Comforter. "When He is come," says our Lord, "He will reprove the world of sin, and of righteousness, and of judgment." Now, has He so come to *you*? Has He been so received by you? Do you receive and accept His reproofs of sin? Do you hunger after the righteousness He holds up before you? Do you humble yourself under the judgment He passes on you? As you do so, and in the measure you do so, and at the times you do so, to that extent and at those times you pass over from the world which knoweth not the Spirit of truth, and you gain the discipleship to which their Master sends the Comforter. Has He, then, the Reprover and the Sanctifier, come to you, and been received by you? That is the first question. That is the *previous* question. Not that it need be feared that the world will be greedy to take to itself the comforts of God's people. It "cannot," says our Lord. For it neither sees those comforts nor knows them. No more it does—when you think of it. What could a man of Babylon have made of the Prophecy of Isaiah? Even the wisest of the men of the East —what could they have made of the evangelical prophet? He would have been "foolishness" to them. They had not, as Paul would say, the mind of Christ. They had not had the experience of a

true Israelite. Babylon was no banishment to
them. Jerusalem had no attractions to them.

Nay,—not only had Jerusalem and her prophets
and her promises no attractions to the men of
Babylon : there were many men of Israel who
turned a deaf ear to the prophet's comforts. It is
a matter of history that multitudes of Israelites
remained in Babylon, and would not face the
wilderness, spite of all that Isaiah and his fellow-
prophets could say. And so it is still. The iron
has not sufficiently entered our hearts. The
bondage has not sufficiently broken our hearts.
The Holy Ghost has not sufficiently come as a
reprover of sin and of righteousness and of
judgment ; and as a consequence we are not prepared for Him as a Comforter. " That the saying
of Esaias the prophet might be fulfilled, which he
spake, Lord, who hath believed our report ? and
to whom hath the arm of the Lord been revealed ? "

2. The first difficulty that the Holy Ghost has
with us is to get His reproof of sin, and His con-
viction of sin, brought home to our hearts. And
then, that accomplished only raises another difficulty—how to get His *comforts* spoken in our
reproved and convicted hearts. The captives,
whose hearts and consciences were in the Babylonian
captivity, raised as many doubts, difficulties,
apprehensions, and obstacles in Isaiah's way as the
disconsolate disciples did in their Master's way : till

Isaiah's answers, till God's answers to their guilty
and fearful hearts have made Isaiah as good as an
apostle of Christ, as good as a preacher of New
Testament consolation. You all know these golden
consolations. " I, even I, am He that blotteth
out thy transgressions for Mine own sake, and will
not remember thy sins. I have blotted out, as a
thick cloud, thy transgressions, and as a cloud thy
sins : return unto Me, for I have redeemed thee.
Look unto Me, and be ye saved, all the ends of the
earth : for I am God, and there is none else. For
a small moment have I forsaken thee : but with
great mercies will I gather thee. In a little wrath
I hid My face from thee for a moment ; but with
everlasting kindness will I have mercy upon thee,
saith the Lord thy Redeemer." These are God's
very own words to us this morning. To all of us,
that is, who have come up to this house reproved
and convinced of sin. " Comfort ye, comfort ye
My people, saith your God. Speak ye comfortably
to Jerusalem, and cry unto her, that her seventy
years are accomplished, and that her iniquity is
pardoned ! "

3. But, let this be said in the same breath with
all that—this caution and correction—that no
man living in any known sin is ever comforted of
God. The Holy Ghost never yet spake one word
of all His abounding consolations to any man so
long as he lived in any actual sin, or in any neglect

of known duty. You have that much-needed caution bound up into the very heart of God's great name, when He proclaimed His great Name to Moses. " The Lord God, merciful and gracious, long-suffering, and abundant in goodness and truth, keeping mercy for thousands, forgiving iniquity and transgression and sin—*but*"—and here comes this great correction and caution—" will by no means clear the guilty." That is to say, as long as you are living in any *guilt*, as long as your conscience accuses you, He will by no means clear or comfort you. "He that forsaketh his sin shall find mercy"— but he only. You do not really care for God's mercy or His comfort either, so long as you live in any sin. And it is well that you do not ; for you can have neither. Your peace will be like a river, when you put away your sin ; but not one word of true peace, not one drop of true comfort, can you have till then. You will have to put out God's eyes, and pervert His judgment, and turn His Throne upside down, before you can have His comfort with your sin. Choose which you will have : " If a man love Me, he will keep My words : and My Father will love him, and We will come unto him, and make Our abode with him." Are *you* that man ? Are you intending to be that man ? And when and in what are you to begin ? Are you from this day to keep that word of His, which up to this day you know you have not kept ?

Then, from this day Jesus and His Father will come to your good and honest, if broken and contrite heart, and will make Their abode with you. And from this memorable day it will be said over you from heaven, what was said from heaven in Israel over all the men in Israel like you : " To this man will I look, saith the Lord, even to him that is poor and of a contrite spirit, and who trembleth at My word."

4. This is the rule, then, that comfort comes with obedience. But there are exceptions to every rule ; and God's rules with His people are full of exceptions. His people are so full of idiosyncrasy, non-conformity, and originality that no rule could possibly be laid down that would cover them all, or indeed, any two of them all. And hence it is that God has to make as many rules in His sanctification and comfort of His people as He has people to sanctify and comfort. Every new addition made to God's people has a new rule made for itself. Heman [1] and Job are great favourites with the profounder of the Puritan case-preachers. Heman and Job were famous exceptions to the common rule that comfort comes with obedience. And you may possibly be a New Testament Job or Heman. You may, like them, have been chosen of God on a special platform on which God is going to display some deep and sovereign exception to

[1] See the title of Ps. lxxxviii.

His usual manner of dealing with His people.
That may be so; but you will be well advised not
to assume that too much till you have proved it
true by a lifetime of strict and spiritual obedience.
And then, if, after a lifetime of strict and spiritual
obedience, you are still left without your promised
and expected comfort—why—then you are in good
company, and must not complain. " God gives
grace," says Goodwin, " in cases where He does
not give comfort; and then, He is the God of all
grace in a far larger extent than of all comfort:
yea, and often He gives most grace when He gives
least comfort. He carries on some souls—as He
carried on Christ at His death—*i.e.* to the highest
acts of obedience, whilst yet He vouchsafes no
comfort. Witness that doleful expression of
Christ: ' My God, My God, why hast Thou forsaken Me ? '—when yet He was in the highest act
of obedience. Thus in thy temptation God will
influence thee with grace, secretly assisting and
strengthening thee, even when He affords thee no
sensible comfort. Carry this home with thee,"
adds the great preacher comfortably—" Carry this
home with thee, thou who hast for so many years
been tossed with tempest and not comforted."

5. " Oh," some of you will say in answer to all
that—" you speak of exceptions, but I am an
exception in nothing but in the corruption of my
heart. How could God or man comfort a heart

like mine ? No man sees my heart, else all men
would flee from me. And it is because God sees
my heart that He has so forsaken me. Do not
speak about comfort to me ! I want no comfort :
I want—if God would give it and could give it—
I want a clean heart : *that,* as God is my witness,
would be comfort enough for me. I want the
devil and hell taken out of my heart," you protest.
Your only moments of comfort are not when your
corn and wine abound, but when the devil is asleep
for a season. " O, wretched man that I am ! I
am of all men the most miserable ! " Yes ! and
No ! You *are* ; and you are *not.* I will tell you
a far greater misery than yours, and a far greater
wretchedness. It is a great deal worse misery to
be miserable and not to know it. To be poor, and
miserable, and blind, and naked, and to think, all
the time, that you are rich and increased with
goods and have need of nothing. At your worst,
that is not your misery. If to know your misery is
any alleviation of it, then surely that alleviation
is yours. If to know nothing but misery is any
preparation for God's mercy—as it is—then according to your own showing and out of your own
mouth, who among us all is prepared for God's
mercy this day like you ? There is only one
Scripture you ever get any comfort out of. This is
your text every morning, and you come back to it
every night. " The good that I would, I do not,"

you say, " but the evil which I would not, that I
do." Very good. But, come on! Come on, and
complete your own scripture—" I find, then, a law
that when I would do good, evil is present with me."
And come on still—" For I delight in the law of
God after the inward man. O wretched man!"
you cry of your own accord, yes; but there is
more—" I thank God through Jesus Christ my
Lord. There is therefore now no condemnation";
and ere ever you are aware, you will be swimming
in a sea of comfort, a sea without a bottom or a
shore. You are launched upon the eighth of the
Romans, and into the ocean of comfort, out of
which that great chapter is but a cup.

6. You would let go; you would yield yourself
up on the spot to any of God's comforts He or His
servants are pleased to speak to you this day—if it
were not that you are such an atheist and scandal
in prayer. But your conscience is so in prison
about prayer that you feel as if you must flee from
the Lord's table. Bad as your heart is, and bad as
your life has been, yet there is nothing that makes
you feel so despicable and so castaway as your
shameful neglect of prayer. You like to read
books about prayer. You like to hear sermons
about prayer. You reverence and love the men
of prayer. But all that only makes you a greater
beast before God. You are in positive despair
about prayer. And yet, you know on the testi-

mony of thousands, and on the assurance of God's
word in endless places—that prayer is, of all things
a mortal man can perform, by far the most blessed.
How can prophet, or apostle, or the Holy Ghost
Himself, comfort you ? You refuse to be comforted ! The greatest and the best of comforts is
in your own house, is every day, morning and night,
and seven times a day, in your own heart ; and you
will not move a hand or foot to take it. There is
no mystery about prayer : no mystery, but its
nearness, and its easiness, and its sureness, and
its fruitfulness, and its supreme, immediate, and
everlasting blessedness. Only begin to pray.
Prayer, of all things, only needs a beginning.
Begin, and it will beat you to give over. Begin,
and you will be a man of prayer yourself before
you know where you are,—a man of power with
God, and not only a greatly comforted man yourself, but a fountainhead of comfort to many others.
What a father you would then begin to be and what
a mother ! What a sister and what a brother !
What a friend and what a lover ! What a minister
and what a member ! For you would have a well
of comfort springing up in your own heart ; and
out of your heart comfort would flow like a river,
far and near round about you. Till you, even you
would be found exclaiming with Paul : " God
comforteth us in all our tribulation, that we may
be able to comfort them that are in any trouble,

by the comfort wherewith we ourselves are comforted of God." " You will comfort My people," saith your God to His servants, " if you could prevail with them to pray." We shall do our best, O God! Only pour out on us all, prophets and people, the promised spirit of prayer and supplication!

7. But the Lord's Supper is the crown and the seal of all our best comforts in this life. And you will never be nearer the " God of all comfort " till you sit down with Him in heaven, than you will be immediately, in a few moments. " I sat," says the Bride, " under His shadow with great delight, and His fruit was sweet to my taste. He brought me into His banqueting-house, and His banner over me was love."

> " Thou art coming to a King ;
> Large petitions with thee bring :
> For His grace and power are such,
> None can ever ask too much."

2

THE EVANGELICAL PROPHET

" Who hath believed our report ? "—Isa. liii. 1.

It was when Jerome was engaged in translating this chapter out of its original Hebrew into his western Latin, that he exclaimed in wonder and in praise: " Surely this is the chapter of a New Testament evangelist, rather than of an Old Testament prophet ! " And ever since Jerome said that, Isaiah has been known in the Church as " The Evangelical Prophet." " Not only many Jews," says Albert Bengel, " but even atheists have been converted to Jesus Christ by means of this chapter. History records the names of some of them : God alone knows the names of them all." And John Donne says that as " in the New Testament we have ' The Gospel according to Matthew,' and ' The Gospel according to Mark,' and ' The Gospel according to Luke,' and ' The Gospel according to John ' : so in the Old Testament we have ' The Gospel according to Isaiah.' " " The fifty-third of Isaiah reads," says Delitzsch, " as if it had

been written beneath the Cross of Calvary. This
chapter is the most central chapter, the deepest
and the highest chapter, in the whole of the Old
Testament. The Holy Ghost has here excelled
Himself," says Delitzsch.

And indeed, this most wonderful chapter deserves
all, and more than all, that has ever been said in
admiration of it. The Old Testament believers cast
their surest anchors on this Scripture. They had
more anchorages than this ; but this was the surest,
the safest, and the most consoling anchorage of
them all. There is nothing, indeed, like this
chapter even in the New Testament itself : there
is no other single scripture—in the whole of the
Word of God—in which the sin-atoning death of
the Son of God is set before the faith of a sinner as
it is here. Simply nowhere else is the redeeming
death of Christ set forth so clearly, so fully, so
emphatically, so explicitly, so positively, so experi-
mentally, so impossibly-to-be-disputed, and so
impossibly-to-be-for-one-moment-doubted—as it is
here. A sinner must have his eyes sealed up very
close indeed, not to see his salvation here. He
must surely have a very seared conscience, who
does not flee to the Cross of Christ as it stands so
open to him in this chapter. Listen, again, to the
accumulated statements of the atonement in this
single scripture : listen, and cast your anchor on
every one of them, as I repeat them to you for that

purpose. " He hath borne our griefs, and carried our sorrows : He was stricken, smitten of God, and afflicted : He was wounded for our transgressions, He was bruised for our iniquities : the chastisement of our peace was upon Him ; and with His stripes we are healed. All we like sheep have gone astray ; we have turned every one to his own way ; and the Lord hath laid on Him the iniquity of us all. He was oppressed, and He was afflicted, yet He opened not His mouth : He is brought as a lamb to the slaughter, and as a sheep before her shearers is dumb, so He openeth not His mouth. . . . For the transgression of my people was He stricken. . . . It pleased the Lord to bruise Him ; He hath put Him to grief : when Thou shalt make His soul an offering for sin . . . He shall bear their iniquities : . . . because He hath poured out His soul unto death ; and He was numbered with the transgressors ; and He bare the sin of many, and made intercession for the transgressors."

All the other Scriptures of the Old Testament are written with pen and ink ; but these things read as if they were written with the very blood of Christ Himself, with the sin-atoning blood of the Lamb of God slain for Old Testament believers, and New, before the foundation of the world.

" The Lord hath laid on Him the iniquity of us all." Could any conceivable language be clearer ? What more, what better for us could possibly have

been said ? Nothing better : unless it is the
margin, where it is said : " The Lord hath made
the iniquity of us all to meet on Him." Now, my
brethren, though it is not too much for Almighty
God, and His Divine Son, to take up and deal with
the iniquity of us all, it is impossible for us to take
up all that iniquity into our minds, and to lay it
all upon our hearts. And it is not intended, nor
expected, that we should do so. What we are
called to think of and to deal with here is our own
individual iniquity, and to think of it as taken
off us and laid upon Jesus Christ. We shall simply
lose ourselves, we shall simply drown ourselves, if
we begin with the iniquity of all other men, and
try to wade out into that ocean, and into our Lord's
atoning death for all that. The right way is to
begin and end with our own iniquities, and with
our Lord's atoning death for us and for them.
The right way is to read this great Scripture, as if
it were written for, and addressed to, each single
one of us separately and alone ; and as if there
were no other sinful man for Christ to die for in
the whole world, but ourselves. " Hast thou
believed our report ? "—this demand is made to
each one of us, severally and alone. " Has the
arm of the Lord been revealed to thee ? Has the
Lord made all thine iniquities to meet on His
substituted Son ? " The whole Atonement—in all
its length, and breadth, and height, and depth—is

far too high, and far too deep for us. It is enough
for us to have to make sure that our own iniquities
have all been atoned for, and that the Son of God
has taken them all for ever away, and has given
us His own justifying righteousness in their place.

And as it is our own sins and iniquities that we
are to think of when the report of the atonement is
made to us, even so it is certain particular sins and
transgressions of our own that we are to think of.
We are not to attempt to think of the mass and the
immensity of our sins, for that also is far too much
for us. A long lifetime of sin, and then our whole
nature steeped and soaked in sin,—what human
mind could keep all that in memory, or could ever
take up and feel aright the full weight and guilt
and shame of all that ? No human mind, no
human heart could ever do so. It is absolutely
impossible. But it is possible to take this and that
sin, this and that transgression, and to lay it on
our offered Surety and Substitute. " Innumerable
evils compass us all about," and pursue us like so
many avengers of blood. But it is not our innumerable evils that we are always to deal with,
so much as that evil, and that evil, and that other
evil : committed at that time, and at that place,
and against that person, God or man. It is this
and that particular evil and special sin that we are
to fix our eyes on, as the Lord takes it, and lays it
on His sin-bearing Son.

And then, when we do that—how our sins horrify
us at such times, and make us at such times to hate
them almost as much as God Himself hates them!
To have to take this and that sin, in all its vileness
and wickedness, and to have to stand and see it
taken off ourselves, and laid on the sinless head of
the Son of God.   Oh, my brethren — why does
that not break our hearts in pieces, never to be
healed again?   Why does that not make it impossible for us ever to perpetrate that sin again?
Oh, the fearful dominion of sin!   Oh, the unspeak-
able deceitfulness and persistence of sin!   That
it can still survive such awful experience as that!
And that it can still steal away our hearts from
such a God and such a Saviour!   But hard and all
but hopeless as our hearts are—yet every time we
do attempt to take such and such a sin and to lay
it on Another, and on such Another—as a matter
of fact that does do something to horrify our hearts
at that sin, and at the thought of loading and
defiling and crucifying the Son of God again with
that sin.   But in His mercy, God tempers and
softens our sight of our sin, and of His Son's death
for our sin; else we would lose our reason at the
awful sight.   All the same—soften it as He may—
it remains absolutely true, — as true as God is
true; as true as Christ is true; as true as the
Gospel is true, — that the Lord hath laid on
Him all our iniquities, all the most abominable,

and the most aggravated of our iniquities and our transgressions.

And then, what a cruel catalogue of our Lord's sufferings for our sins, this prophet here reads home upon our broken hearts! " His visage, marred more than any man, and His form more than the sons of men. Stricken, smitten, wounded, bruised, chastised, scourged, oppressed, afflicted." And every accursed syllable of all that—" for me." Nothing of all that would ever have come near Him, but for me. All that was my desert. All that was the wages of my sin. But for Him, and His interposition, and His substitution of Himself, my visage would have been marred more than any man. But for Him, I would have been despised and rejected of men, and no man would ever have put any esteem upon me. I would have been stricken, smitten of God, and afflicted. I would have been wounded, and bruised, and chastised, and scourged. I would have had all mine iniquity laid on myself. I would have been oppressed and afflicted; I would have been bruised and put to grief! That, communicants, is the way for you and me to go through this expiation-scripture. That is the way for a man to examine himself and so to eat of that bread and drink of that cup. That is the way to "receive the atonement." That is the way so to make Christ our sin that we may be made His righteousness. That is the way to let Him see of the travail of His soul,—that it has not been wholly lost and altogether thrown away upon us. " I, O Esaias ! I, for one, have believed thy report ! To me, for one, has the arm of the Lord been revealed ! "—so let us all say, and each man, for himself.

Among the many amazing things of which this amazing chapter is full, there is nothing that arrests us, and overawes us, and, indeed, staggers us more than this—that it " pleased the Lord to bruise " His Messiah-Son. But the simple truth of God in this matter is this. God was so set, from ever-lasting, on the salvation of sinners that the most awful steps that had to be taken in order to work out that salvation are here said to have absolutely pleased Him. It is somewhat like our Lord's own words—" I delight to do Thy will " : even when His Father's will led Him to the garden of Geth-semane and the Cross of Calvary. God so loved the world that He gave up His only-begotten Son to die for the sin of the world. God could not be pleased with the death of His Son—in itself. No. But nothing has ever pleased Him more than that His Son should lay down His life in atonement for those sinners whom the Father had chosen and ordained to everlasting life. Paul has everything. And he has the Father's indebtedness to His Son and His good pleasure in His death in this great passage : " God hath set forth Christ Jesus to be a

propitiation through faith in His blood : to declare
His righteousness, that He might be just and the
justifier of him which believeth in Jesus." It
pleased the Lord to bruise Him, because in this way
alone could God's full hatred of sin be declared to
men and angels, and at the same time God's justice
might be manifested in the salvation of sinners.
Yes; " Esaias is very bold " when he says that
" it pleased the Lord to bruise Him." But in
saying that, Esaias is not one word bolder than is
the whole of the glorious Gospel, in its proclamation
of God's supremest glory in the death of Christ, and
in the consequent salvation of sinners, and a multitude of such that no man can number. As one
of the greatest preachers of the Gospel that ever
lived has it : " For God to deliver up His Son to
death, and for Himself to bruise Him, and that this
should be His good pleasure : there must have been
some incomprehensibly vast design of glory to
accrue therefrom and to be only attained by doing
it : some high end, and far transcending design,
that was to be the issue and the product of it ; and
which, as you know, was the manifestation and
magnifying of His grace in the salvation of sinners.
And this is surely the very highest evidence and
argument to our faith that can possibly be given—
that God is determined to save sinners. For what
has been done to Christ is for ever past recalling ;
and is not to be justified or recompensed in any

14

other way, than by saving many by the knowledge
of Him—as God here speaks by the mouth of His
prophet."

" Yet it pleased the Lord to bruise Him: He
hath put Him to grief : when Thou shalt make His
soul an offering for sin, He shall see His seed, He
shall prolong His days, and the pleasure of the
Lord shall prosper in His hand." Now this is the
conclusion of this whole matter—for this morning :
Does He see His seed in us ? In you and in me ?
If He does, then He is " satisfied " for all the
" travail of His soul "—so far as we are concerned.
He forgets and forgives all His sufferings when He
sees His seed ; when He sees the souls He has
redeemed to God with His own blood, putting on
His image, and filled with His Spirit, and continuing
His work in this world. Now—in closing—let us
look back into this great chapter as into a glass,
in order to see if we can recognise any of the features
and characteristics of Christ in ourselves,—any of
those features and characteristics of Christ as they
are here so impressively set forth to our faith, and
to our love, and to our imitation. As thus : " He
is despised and rejected of men : a man of sorrows
and acquainted with grief : He was despised and
we esteemed Him not." Now as to the bearing of
all that upon us, the Apostle Peter has spoken to
all time. And this is what he has said : " For
hereunto were ye called : because Christ also

suffered for us, leaving us an example, that ye should follow His steps : Who, when He was reviled, reviled not again : when He suffered, He threatened not." Now, how do you stand in these matters ? For, every day and every hour, God so orders things around some of you, and so brings things to bear upon some of you, that you are buffeted and reviled and despised and rejected—almost every day. And that, for this very purpose that at such times Christ shall see His seed in you. Now, does He ? You know your own heart under all that discipline ; and He knows it. Now, does He see in your heart at such times of temptation and trial a copy of His own ? " A copy, Lord, of Thine."

Then again : you will sometimes be wounded for other people's transgressions, as He was for yours. And " bruised for their iniquities," as He was for yours. Now—how about your speech or your silence under all that ? " He opened not His mouth." How happy you are, and how much to be envied, if you are His seed in that also. To suffer injury and pain, and shame and humiliation—at home and abroad, and never to retaliate, or to let it be seen that you suffer so acutely. Happy communicant ! the seed and the solace of Christ if that is so ! My brethren, almost above everything else in this world, imitate Christ in His silence. For, " the tongue can no man tame." No man, but the Man of Sorrows. But He can. He tamed the tongue in Himself, and He is taming it in you—if you are indeed His seed. More and more imitate Him, then, amid all the injuries and insults, and provocations, and vexations, and even annoyances, that are let loose upon you every day—and for this very end—that your Redeemer may see His seed in you and in your silence under injuries and wrongs. " For, hereunto also are ye called."

" Neither was any deceit in His mouth." Now, cleanse your mouth also of all duplicity and double-mindedness. Be sincere and simple ; and in everything and to every man be honest and honour-able. Let your yea be yea, and your nay, nay. Till the God of all truth and all integrity shall see His true children in you, and till the Son of God shall see His true seed in you.

And, to sum up : " He was numbered with the transgressors : and He bare the sin of many, and made intercession for the transgressors." This is the crowning grace of Christ—both in Messianic prophecy and in its evangelical fulfilment—" He made intercession for the transgressors," and especially for those who had transgressed against Himself. Do you the same ! Shut your door, and do the same ! Make intercession for those who will never know it till the books are opened—that you may be the children of your Father which is in heaven ; and that Christ Jesus may be the First-born among many such brethren as you. " For as many as are led by the Spirit of God "—in such things as these—" they are the sons of God. The Spirit also bearing witness with our Spirit, that we are the children of God. And, if children, then heirs, heirs of God, and joint heirs with Christ : if so be that we suffer with Him, that we may be also glorified together."

3

THE RANSOM

" To give His life a ransom for many."—MATT. xx. 28.

LET us draw near this morning and join ourselves to our Lord when He is on His way up to the Passover for the last time. And let us abide near Him this morning till we see the end. And when we see the end, let us all say for ourselves what Paul said for himself: " He loved me and gave Himself for me."

1. No sooner had our Lord entered Jerusalem in the beginning of that week than, in His own words, He began " to give His life a ransom." As long as His time had not yet come, our Lord took great care of His life. His was the most precious life on the face of the earth, and He took corresponding care of it. But now that the work of His life was finished, He began at once to give His life away. All the beginning and middle of that Passover week our Lord was preaching all the daytime in the temple—and then at night He went out and abode in the Mount that is called the Mount of Olives. All that week, our Lord preached all

day and prayed all night. Now there is nothing
so exhausting as preaching unless it is praying:
such preaching, that is, and such praying as our
Lord's preaching and praying were all that Passover week. Paul in one place speaks about preaching the "terror of the Lord." And that terrible
word best describes our Lord's last sermons in
Jerusalem. It is remarkable—and there must be
a good reason for it—that the only sermons of our
Lord that we have anything like a full report of are
His first sermon and His last,—His Sermon on the
Mount and His three days of farewell sermons in
the temple. That preacher was simply throwing
his life away who delivered the discourses that
Matthew has preserved in the end of his Gospel.
He was walking straight into the jaws of death
who stood up in the temple—especially when there
was not standing room in its passover-porches, and
spoke the parable of "The Wicked Husbandman,"
and the parable of "The Marriage Feast," and the
parable of "The Ten Virgins," and the parable of
"The Last Judgment." And then, to make it
impossible that His meaning could be missed, He
hurled out such bolts of judgment as these: "Woe
unto you, Scribes and Pharisees: hypocrites!
Woe! Woe! Woe!" For three whole days the
terrible Preacher was permitted to anticipate the
Last Day; and no man laid hands on Him. And
then, all night in the Mount of Olives, our Lord,

all that week, was simply squandering away what
remained of His life. Unless, indeed, He was in
all that ransoming the lost lives of those preachers
who tune their pulpits ; and who, once they are
home from their day's work and have well dined,
will not venture out again after either to preach
or to pray. The Son of Man gave His life for many
ministers, in the temple and in the garden, as well
as on the tree.

2. The calmness of mind and the careful delibera-
tion with which our Lord goes about the Last Supper
is very affecting and very impressive. The quiet
and orderly way in which He gives his instructions
about the Supper ; the serene and stately way
in which He performs His whole part in the Upper
Room ; the watchful solicitude He shows about
the behaviour of the disciples both to Himself and
to one another, while all the time His own terrible
death was just at the door,—it melts our hearts
to see it all. He dwells on the Supper. He lingers
over the Supper. He lengthens it out. He takes
it up, part after part. He looks back at Moses in
Egypt. He looks forward to the marriage-supper
of the Lamb. He legislates for the future of His
ransomed Church and people. He takes the paschal
lamb out of the Supper, and He puts Himself in its
place. "Take, eat, this is My body broken for you.
This is My blood of the New Testament," said the
Lamb of God, "shed for many, for the remission of

sins : drink ye all of it. And do this till I come."
What a heart-melting sight ! What nobleness !
What peace ! What beauty of holiness ! What
boundless love !

3. " Then cometh Jesus with them to a place
called Gethsemane, and saith to the disciples, Sit
ye there, while I go and pray yonder." Our Lord
is in no mood for mockery ; but our hearts read
their own bitterness into His departing words. He
seeks out a seat for the disciples. He seeks out the
best, the softest, and the most sheltered seat in the
garden. He points them to the place, and He bids
them sit down in it. He tells them to keep near
one another, and to keep one another company.
And before He has got to His place " yonder," they
are all fast asleep ! *He* has not slept for a week.
Night after night He has spent in that same spot,
till even Judas " knew the place." More than
the city watchmen for the morning He had waited
for God in that garden all that week ; and He still
waits. " Out of the depths have I cried to Thee, O
Lord. Out of the belly of hell, O Lord. Then I
said, I am cast out of Thy sight. The waters com-
passed me about even to the soul : the weeds were
wrapped about my head." And being in an agony,
He prayed more earnestly ; and His sweat was as
it were great drops of blood falling to the ground.
It was the wages of sin. It was the Lord laying
on Him the iniquities of us all. It was—every

ransomed soul knows what it was. " Yes ; it was
my cup," says every ransomed soul. " I mingled
it, I filled it, I have sometimes just tasted it. No
wonder He loathed it. No wonder He put it away.
No wonder He sweat blood as He drank it. For
that cup was *sin*. It was the wages of my sin. It
was full of the red wine of the wrath of God against
me." And when He rose off His face and left the
trampled-down and blood-soaked winepress, He
found the disciples still sleeping. And again our
hearts mock at us as He says, " Sleep on now, and
take your rest."

4. Were you ever false as hell to your best friend ?
Did you ever take your unsuspecting friend by the
hand and say, Welcome ! or Farewell ? Was there
ever a sweet smile on your face, while there was a
dagger under your cloak ? Did envy, or ambition,
or revenge, or some such pure and downright devil
ever enter your heart—till you almost went out
and hanged yourself with horror at yourself ?
Then thou art the man that Jesus Christ ransomed
from the halter and from hell when He submitted
His cheek to the kiss of the traitor. It is because
Jesus Christ has you and so many like you among
His disciples that He took so meekly the diabolical
embrace of the son of perdition. " It was not an
enemy that reproached me : then I could have
borne it : neither was it he that hated me that
did magnify himself against me : then would I

have hid myself from him. But it was thou, a
man, mine equal, my guide and mine acquaintance.
We took sweet counsel together, and walked into
the house of God in company. Yea, mine own
familiar friend, in whom I trusted, which did eat
of my bread, hath lifted up his heel against me."
" For we ourselves were sometimes living in malice
and envy, hateful and hating one another. But
after that the kindness and love of God our Saviour
toward man appeared—not by works of righteousness which we have done, but according to His
mercy He saved us, by the washing of regeneration
and the renewing of the Holy Ghost: which He shed
on us abundantly, through Jesus Christ our Saviour,
that being justified by His grace, we should be made
heirs according to the hope of eternal life."

5. " Then the band, and the captain and the
officers of the Jews, took Jesus and bound Him."
It is a very bitter moment to a prisoner when the
officers of justice are binding him. I have often
thought that the pinioning before execution must
be almost more dreadful than the very drop itself.
And our Lord felt most acutely the shame and the
disgrace of the prison shackles. For once He broke
silence and spoke out and remonstrated. " Be ye
come out as against a thief ? " He turned upon the
officers. He had no intention of trying to escape.
He had come out to the garden to give Himself up.
He had said just the moment before, " I am He:

take Me; and let these go their way." But the officers were under the instructions of Judas. Their superiors in the city had told them that they were to look to Judas for all their orders that night. And Judas had said to the officers: "Whomsoever I shall kiss, that same is He: take Him and lead Him away safely: that same is He, hold Him fast." And they obeyed Judas; they held Him as fast and as safe as their best prison-cords could hold Him. O officers! officers! Judas must surely know; but it is impossible that you can know why it is that your prisoner walks with you so willingly! Did any of you Roman officers ever hear of "cords of love?" Well,—it is in the cords of everlasting love that you keep your man so safely to-night. O officers! officers! if you only knew who that is you are leading in cords into the city! O Judas, Judas! What are thy thoughts? O! Better never to have been born!

6. "And all His disciples forsook Him and fled. But Peter followed Him afar off, unto the high priest's palace, and went in and sat with the servants to see the end." Did you ever deny a friend? Did you ever sit still and hear a friend of yours slandered, witnessed against by hired witnesses, and condemned? Did you ever sit and warm yourself at some man's fire; or more likely, at some man's wine; and for fear, for cowardice, or for the sake of the company and the good cheer

did you nod and smile and wink away your absent brother's good name ? Look ! redeemed dastard ! look at thy dreadful ransom ! Look at Jesus Christ in the hard hands, and under the hired tongues of His assassins—and Peter, His sworn friend, washing his hands of all knowledge of the friendless Prisoner ! Look ! O dog in the shape of a man ! All their sham charges, all their lying witnesses, all their judicial insults and brutalities are clean forgotten by Peter's Master ! He does not hear what they are saying, and He does not care. A loud voice out in the porch has stabbed our Lord's heart to death. " I know not the Man ! I never saw Him till to-night ! " With oaths and with curses above all the babel—Peter's loud voice rolls in on his Master : " I know not the Man ! " And the cock crew. And the Lord turned and looked upon Peter. And Peter went out and wept bitterly. And as the fine legend has it : Peter never heard a cock crow, day nor night, all his after days, that he did not remember the passover-porch of Caiaphas the High Priest that year in Jerusalem !

7. You have heard sometimes about hell being let loose. Yes, but hear this. Come to Caiaphas' palace on the passover night, and look at this. " Then did they spit in His face, and buffeted Him : they blindfolded Him and then they smote Him with the palms of their hands, saying : Prophesy to

us, Thou Christ, who is it that smote Thee? And
they stripped Him, and put on Him a scarlet robe.
And when they had platted a crown of thorns "—
I wonder in what sluggard's garden it grew!—
" they put it upon His head, and a reed in His
right hand; and they bowed the knee before Him
and mocked Him, saying: Hail! King of the Jews!
And they spit upon Him again, and took the reed
out of His hand, and smote Him upon the head.
Then Pilate took Jesus and scourged Him. After
which they brought Jesus forth wearing the crown
of thorns and the purple robe. And when the
Chief Priests saw Jesus, they cried out, Crucify
Him! crucify Him! Then Pilate delivered Him
to them to be crucified." My brethren,—these are
dreadful, most dreadful, things. And all the time,
God Almighty, the God and Father of Jesus Christ,
restrained Himself; He held Himself in, and sat
as still as a stone, seeing and hearing all that. The
arrest, the trial, the buffeting, the spitting, the
jesting and the jeering, the bloody scourging, the
crown of thorns, the reed, and the purple robe—
Why? In the name of amazement, why did the
Judge of all the earth sit still and see all that said
and done? Do you know what made Him sit still?
Did you ever think about it? And would you
like to be told how it could be? God Almighty,
my brethren, not only sat still, but He ordained
it all; and His Son *endured* it all,—*in order to take*

away sin. In order to take away the *curse* of sin, to take away the very existence of sin for ever. You will find the explanation of that terrible night's work, and of the still more terrible morning just about to dawn,—you will find the explanation, the justification, and the complete key to it all *in your own heart.*

Did you ever see yourself to be such a despicable creature that you wondered why all men did not spit upon you? Did you ever wonder that, not friendship and family life only, but very human society itself, did not dissolve, and fall in pieces, such is the meanness, the despicableness, the duplicity, the selfishness, the cruelty, and the diabolical wickedness of the human heart—but above all human hearts, of yours? You will understand the spitting-scene that night when God lets you see your own heart. There was no surplus shame; there was no scorn too much: the contumely was not one iota overdone that night. There was no unnecessary disgrace poured on Christ that night. They are in every congregation, at every Communion Table, and they are the salt and the ornament of it, who say as they sit down at the Table—He hid not His face from shame and from spitting for me! He loved me in my sin and my shame, and He gave Himself for me!

8. If all that will not melt your heart of stone,

try the next thing that Pilate and his devils did. For Pilate scourged Him. I will leave the scourging to yourselves to picture, and to ask, What is scourging? Who was it that was that morning scourged? And why was He scourged being innocent? And the crown of thorns, and all the awful scene to the end! O that mine head were waters and mine eyes a fountain of tears!

9. But come out to Calvary at nine o'clock that morning if you would be absolutely glutted with sorrow and with love. All the shame, all the scorn, all the horror, all the agony due to our sin, and undertaken by our Surety—it all met on the Cross. The Cross was the vilest, the cruellest, the most disgraceful, the most diabolical instrument of execution that ever hell had invented and set up on earth. Stand back and let the chiefest sinner in this house come forward. Give him the best place. Whoever sees the crucifixion, let *him* see it. Look, sinner, and see. They lay down the Cross on the ground. They then take the cords off our Lord's pinioned arms, and the painted board off His breast. They then lay Him down on His back on the Cross; they stretch out His arms along the arms of the Cross. They then open out His hands; and with a hammer they drive a great nail of iron through His right hand with the blood spurting up in their faces; and another through His left hand, and another through His feet,

placed the one above the other to save the nails.
Five or six strong soldiers then lift up the Cross
with its trembling, bleeding Burden, and sink it
down with a dash into the stone socket, set in the
earth, till all His bones are out of joint. And
" They know not what they do ! " is all He says.
No ; *they* know not, but the chief of sinners now
looking on, he knows. Paul knew : " He loved
me," said Paul, " and gave Himself for me."
Cowper knew.

> " There is a fountain filled with blood
>   Drawn from Immanuel's veins ;
> And sinners, plunged beneath that flood,
>   Lose all their guilty stains."

We often pray that God would " make the bed "
of His dying saints ; and He does it. But that
was the death-bed God made for His dying Son !

But all that, after all, was but the outer porch
of death to our Lord. Gethsemane and Caiaphas
and Pilate and Herod's palace were but the outer
court of the temple. The Cross was the altar ; and
the sacrifice only began to be fully offered about
the sixth hour when there was darkness over all
the earth till the ninth hour. It passeth all under-
standing, and all the power of tongue and pen,
what the Son of God suffered in body and in soul,
during those three dark and silent hours. Only at
the ninth hour Jesus cried with a loud voice, " My
God, My God : why hast Thou forsaken Me ? "

15

And some time after, " It is finished," when He
bowed His head and gave up the ghost.

> " 'Tis finished—was His latest voice :
>   These sacred accents o'er,
> He bowed His head, gave up the ghost,
>   And suffered pain no more.

> 'Tis finished : The Messiah dies
>   For sins, but not His own :
> The great redemption is complete
>   And Satan's power o'erthrown."

" So, after He had taken His garments and was set
down again, He said unto them : Know ye what I
have done to you ? "

Yea, Lord.   Thou hast given Thy life a ransom
for many.   Thou hast loved me and given Thyself
for me !

> " I am not worthy, holy Lord,
>   That Thou shouldst come to me ;
> Speak but the word ; one gracious word
>   Can set the sinner free.

> I am not worthy ; cold and bare
>   The lodging of my soul ;
> How canst Thou deign to enter there ?
>   Speak, Lord ! and make me whole.

> I am not worthy ; yet, my God,
>   How can I say Thee nay,—
> Thee, Who didst give Thy flesh and blood
>   My ransom price to pay ?

> O come, in this sweet morning hour
>   Feed me with food Divine ;
> And fill with all Thy love and power
>   This worthless heart of mine."

4

CRUCIFIED WITH CHRIST

" I am crucified with Christ : nevertheless I live ; yet not I, but Christ liveth in me : and the life which I now live in the flesh I live by the faith of the Son of God, Who loved me, and gave Himself for me."—GAL. ii. 20.

WHAT is this that Paul says : " I am crucified with Christ " ? What does the Apostle really mean ? In what sane and solid sense does he use these hitherto unheard-of words ? Saul of Tarsus, we have his own word for it, had never seen Christ, nor His Cross either. He had not been in Gethsemane with Christ like Peter, nor on Calvary with Him like John. The two thieves might have said, " We were crucified with Christ," but how could Saul of Tarsus say it ? For he was still at home in his own country ; he was only as yet an aspirant to Gamaliel's school when Christ was crucified ; and the crucifixion of Christ was long past before Saul had set a foot in the City of the Crucifixion. In what sense then can he say, and say it so often and so boldly, " I am crucified with Christ " ? My brethren, he says it because he

believes it ; he says it because he has experienced
it, and because he is sure of it, as sure of it as he is
sure that he is alive.   Paul was not only the greatest
preacher of the Cross that ever lived ; he was that
because he was more than that, and better than
that ; for he was the greatest and best believer
the doctrine of the Cross ever had. Peter and
John might hesitate and hedge in preaching fully
and freely the Cross of Christ, and all the doctrines
of grace that depend upon it ; they might dissemble
and dissimulate for fear of them that were of the
circumcision, but Paul never.   He knew what he
said, and he meant it down to the very bottom, all
that he said.   He said it ; and he shook them that
seemed to be pillars in Jerusalem by the way he
said it.   " I am crucified with Christ . . . and
though an angel from heaven were to preach any
other Gospel than the Gospel of a believing sinner's
crucifixion with Christ, let him be accursed.   For
I certify you, brethren, that my Gospel is not after
man.   For I neither received it of man, neither was
I taught it, but by the revelation of Jesus Christ."

What, then, is this Gospel that Paul so immediately learned, and so fully and so faithfully preached ?
What is the Gospel of the Cross, and of a sinner's
crucifixion with Christ upon the Cross ?   No man
need misunderstand or be ignorant of the Apostle's
central doctrine if he wishes to understand it, and
takes any trouble to understand it.   For he makes

it quite plain in every Epistle of his. He preaches
nothing else. He has nothing else to preach.
Another Gospel is not another. There is no other
Gospel. It is to the Cross Paul is leading up in all
his teaching about the law of God, and about the
nature and estate of man ; and it is from the same
Cross he leads his readers down again when he
writes of the new life, the peace, the joy, the strength,
the blessedness of all those who, like himself, have
been crucified with Christ. And all up and down
his splendid Epistles he throws in those glorious
glimpses of his own experiences which make all his
Epistles so everyday-like and experimental, amid
all their sweep and magnificence, and amid all their
height and depth. The seventh of Romans, the
third of Philippians, the whole of the Corinthians
and the Galatians, are full of Christ and His Cross ;
and, at the same time, they are full of Paul and his
crucifixion with Christ, and his consequent " life
unto God." And in this text that autobiographic
Gospel of Paul comes to its most condensed and
most compacted expression.

Paul's first experience of the law of God was a
terrible experience. He tells the tragical story to
the Roman believers, to enforce upon them the
necessity, sweetness, and blessedness of the Cross.
Like a fierce accuser, like a dreadful judge, like a
deadly executioner the law of God all at once fell
upon Paul, fell upon him and haled him to prison

and death and judgment just as he had been wont
to hale the disciples of Christ. But, behold, just
as the executioner's axe was lifted up against Paul,
God Himself interposed and said : " Save : I have
found a ransom." " God," said Paul, speaking of
that time, " God revealed His Son in me," and
revealed Him on His Cross.

And though Christ had been crucified long before
on Calvary, yet Paul saw Him " evidently set
forth " during those three days in Damascus. For
three days the mystery of the Cross was being
opened to Paul ; and I think it likely to certainty
that Paul during those three days went down deeper
into the mystery of Redemption than any mortal
man had ever done before, or has ever done since.
No man can come near that mystery and live : the
man Christ Jesus died as He entered into it ; and
while Paul was having it revealed somewhat unto
him he lay as good as dead. | He was three days
without sight, and did neither eat nor drink. But
during those three dead days he had sights given
him to see, and meat given him to eat, that the
Damascus world around him knew not of. He was
like those mysterious beings in heaven who are
" full of eyes within " ; and with his deep inward
eyes Paul saw, as he lay at the mouth of hell,—he
saw, I say, that which he was brought up from hell,
and taken up into heaven, that he might fully and
fearlessly preach. He saw Jesus Christ, the Son of

God, upon the Cross; and he saw Him there made
sin for him, that he might be made the righteousness
of God in Him. Nor did Paul merely see that Cross,
and lie three days and three nights looking at it.
No. Paul was more than a spectator and a student
of the Cross of Christ. Paul was lifted up upon
the Cross and was himself crucified with Christ.
Whether in the body, or out of the body, Paul
could never tell; but ere ever he was aware, he
was lifted up and lost to law and life and all things
upon that awful, that wondrous, that glorious
Cross. The last thing he remembered was his
being lifted up upon that Cross. He did not remember dying; he did not remember being dead:
the last thing he remembered was, with an awful
boldness, laying and leaving his conscience of sin
on the thorn-crowned head of the crucified One.
And in that dying act Paul's whole life—his guilt,
his condemnation, his curse, his very existence—
was all drunk up by that Cross. Paul was as if he
had never been born during those three terrible
days. After those days were over there arose from
the earth on which Paul had lain, there came down
from the Cross on which Paul was crucified, a man,
a form of a man, in some outward respect not
unlike Paul; but it was not the former Paul at all.
Those Damascus disciples he had come to persecute
trembled when they saw Paul, as they thought,
on their streets and in their synagogue, but there

was no cause : the Paul they had heard of was dead, and his world would see him no more. He was dead, and his bones were scattered at the grave's mouth. So effectually, so completely, so utterly did Paul die on the Cross with Christ. Now, do not delude yourselves, and say that this was all an imagination, Paul's powerful and evangelical imagination. No. All this is as real as life and death are real ; as law and justice, judgment and eternity, God and Christ are real. Paul's unreal and imagined life was when he was yet at Gamaliel's school, and on the road to Damascus. After he fell from his horse he came to himself ; he became sane and wise for the first time, and this earth has never seen a saner, wiser, nobler man than Paul the Apostle who was crucified with Christ.

Only, let Luther utter a caution to us here. And let him utter his caution out of that book of which John Bunyan said that he preferred it before all the books he had ever seen as most fit for a wounded conscience. " Paul," says Luther, commenting on this very text, " Paul speaks not here of crucifying by imitation or example, for to follow the example of Christ is also to be crucified with Him. This crucifying is not that of which Peter speaks, that Christ left us an example that we should follow in his steps. But Paul speaketh here of that high crucifying, whereby sin, and the devil, and death are crucified in Christ, and not in me. Here Christ

doth all Himself alone. But I, believing in Christ,
am by faith also crucified with Christ, so that sin,
and death, and the devil, are all crucified and dead
unto me." In Bunyan's day the books that taught
this doctrine were like to fall to pieces if one did but
turn them over! Such books were then the meat
and drink of heroes ; they were the consolation and
the strength of saints.

"I am crucified with Christ : nevertheless I
live." "This is a great mystery even to myself,"
says Paul, "but I will tell you how it has been
fulfilled in me. When the law of God came home
to me I saw that I was a dead man. I saw that the
wages of sin like mine was death. But just then
it was that God in His grace to me revealed His
Son in me. Revealed Him in me a very mystery of
godliness ; revealed Him as made sin, as crucified
for sin, and thus as the Ransom and Redeemer of my
soul. Had I died for my own sin, which I was just
about to do, I had died for ever : I had died the
first and the second death. But dying in and with
Christ, I both died and yet lived. One with Him
in His death, I began again to live in His resurrection life. I awoke off and after the Cross, and found
myself a new creature : old things had passed away,
and all things had become new. I am still dead
to some things,—dead and never to see resurrection.
I am dead to the law, and the law is dead to me.
The law still sometimes looks at me as if it knew me,

and had something against me, and was about to bring up something against me ; but after a time it only looks at me and passes by me. At such moments I tremble to my very heart ; but at such moments God again reveals His Son in me, and I am enabled to say : Why art thou disquieted in me, O my soul ? thou and I are crucified with Christ !

" Nevertheless I live. I live, I say, yet I so live that it is not I that live, but rather it is Christ that liveth in me. In some ways I am the same man I was before I was crucified with Christ, and in some ways I am not. In some not unimportant ways I am the same man, and in some more important ways I am not. My hands and my feet are the same hands and feet I had before I was crucified with Christ ; and yet even they are not quite the same, for they henceforth bear in them the marks of the Lord Jesus. The outward man is much the same ; but the inward man has had a wonderful experience. I was a dead man, a mere corpse and carcass of a man, when the Lord Jesus came to me, and breathed His own life into me, and said unto me, Saul, Saul, receive thou the Holy Ghost ! And I arose and stood upon my feet a living man. I lived, yet not I, but at that moment Christ lived in me."

The next clause is just a repetition, an explanation, and an expansion of what he has already said : " The life which I now live in the flesh I live by the faith of the Son of God." " The life which I now live in the flesh " just means this life you see me live among you, this life of Paul upon the earth, and among the churches, this life of continually travelling about, now east and now west, alternately preaching and tent-making, establishing Churches and writing Epistles. Beneath all that, and behind all that, there lies and works in me this great Gospel mystery of life and death, crucifixion and resurrection, justification and sanctification. I bear about with me daily, in doing all this, the dying of the Lord Jesus ; and the life of Jesus is, at the same time, I trust, somewhat made manifest in my mortal body. For this life I now live in the flesh and on the earth, and till I go to be with Christ which is far better,—this present life I live by faith in the Son of God. My life is not led in obedience to the law : the law and I are for ever done with one another. I have said in every Epistle of mine that I am dead to the law ; and in this matter I do not write one thing, and live another. I do not build again the things I destroyed. Let this be known then as the first article of my creed, and not more my creed than my practice. I, Paul, am dead to the law, and the law to me. So much so that even where I seem to you to obey and not to break the law, it is not the law I obey at all, for I am dead to it. If obedience to the law comes about by my faith in Christ, good and well. But

the law I am under, and the law I obey, is the law
and life of Jesus Christ.   Holiness itself, complete
and spotless holiness, would not win me back to the
law, or reconcile me to its dominion, or authority,
or rewards.   I would not have holiness and Eternal
Life by the law even if it were offered me.   I have
suffered too much from the law ever again to trust it :
no law for me any more !   Christ, and Christ alone,
is lawgiver and righteousness, power and truth,
strength and salvation, temporal and eternal life
to me !   He is " made of God to me wisdom, and
righteousness, and sanctification, and redemption."
I am complete in Him, and the law will never more
find me among its disciples, its devotees, or its
debtors.   For I, through the law, am dead to the
law, that I might live unto God !—unto God, by
faith in His Son,—His Son, I say, Who loved me
and gave Himself for me.

The law never loved me, nor gave a hair of its
head for me.   Even when I obeyed it above many
my equals in my own nation, all the time it never
loved me.) And then, when I, in its least commandment, inadvertently and unconsciously broke it,
it turned upon me with its bowels of brass and its
flaming sword.   But, O the depth of the grace of
God !   I see now that the Son of God loved me even
when I was dead in trespasses and sins ; and I now
love Him because He first loved me.   And if you
speak of commandments and of obedience and of the

law, I will keep all His commandments and all His
law, and obey Him, because He first loved me and
gave Himself for me. I love Him now, and He
knows it ; but He loved me first : He was before-
hand with His love. It was His part and privilege
to love me first. He was the Son and He loved me,
and revealed to me the age and the depth and the
strength of His love, and by all that He carried my
heart captive, and keeps it captive in a willing,
a holy, and an everlasting captivity. Me ! Ay,
me ! " Me,—He loved me," says Paul. Paul does
not grudge or deny or forget the love of Christ to
Peter, or James, or John, or the Galatian believers.
At another time he will write to them about that,
and will powerfully commend the love of Christ to
their hearts ; but what he has before him to-day
is this that Christ loved him, loved Paul himself—
yes, Paul himself. For the time Paul takes the
whole of Christ's love to himself, the whole of
Christ's heart, the whole of His Cross, the whole
of His atoning death, the whole of His blood, and
the whole of His Righteousness.

" He loved me and gave Himself for me." Paul
is back again in a moment at the Cross of Christ.
The mere mention of Christ's love to Paul brings
back the thought of his sin with a rush of darkness
upon his heart, and a rush of blood to his cheek ;
and before he can finish the verse, he has to go back
to the Cross of Christ, and finish it there. He gave

Himself for me, says Paul,—for me and for my sins.
Not for sin, not for the sin of the world, but for the
sin of Paul. For the sin that made Paul all his
days the chief of sinners, and kept him all his days
the least of all saints :—for that sin that was the
thorn of Satan in his flesh, and the sword of God
in his bones, and the sting of death as often as he
thought of death—for me and for my sins. And
then this great verse returns upon itself, returns
upon the Cross, and is locked into a golden chain
of salvation, holding Christ and Paul in one bundle
of life for ever :—one Cross, one Crucifixion, one
Blood, one Righteousness, one Death, one Life, one
Father, and one everlasting Home with Him. " I
am crucified with Christ, . . . Who loved me, and
gave Himself for me."

Now, what bearing has all this on our circumstances and prospects here to-day ? Much bearing,
my brethren : in many ways, and in this way.
For one thing—the law will be sure to cross over
and intrude itself into the province of grace this
day. The law will thrust itself into many an evil
conscience this day. It will stand with its flaming
sword at the door of the table to-day, and will say
to some of you : What dost thou here ? Thou art
a sinner. What hast thou to do to take God's
covenant into thy mouth ? Take care, it will say,
lest God strike thee dead while yet the cup is in
thy unclean hand ! What dost thou here, thou

chief of sinners? And it will fling in thy face some of thy worst sins, and will defy thee to come to the table.

Now what, in that case, are you to do? Do you know what to do? Hast thou learned of Paul what to do at such a solemn moment? I will tell thee what to do. Have thy New Testament open at this text. Place thy finger upon this text, and take heart and say: All thou sayest about me, O accusing law, is all true. But I come here this day on another title and token than thou canst either give me, or take away from me. I come here into His house on the token and invitation and command of Jesus Christ. I come because He said: If ye love Me, this do in remembrance of Me. And I will not go back till He turns me back Himself. Nay, though He seemed to turn me back, I would not believe my eyes. Though He said, " Friend, how camest thou hither?" though He said, "Let the children first be filled"; and even though He said, " Bind him hand and foot "—while they so bind me I will still say: " Just and true are Thy ways, Thou King of Saints; but Thou knowest all things, and Thou knowest that I love Thee!" Say that: I have told thee what to say.

5

TO THE UTTERMOST

"Able to save to the uttermost."—HEB. vii. 25.

"THE uttermost" is the strongest and the extremest word in all the world. There cannot be anything beyond the uttermost. The uttermost is situated on the very extremest rim, and on the very outmost edge, of all existing things. All existence absolutely ends, and comes to its everlasting limit, when it comes to its uttermost. Beyond the uttermost, blank annihilation and sheer nothingness alone exist. We may labour the thought, and we may repeat and multiply the word, till we are wearied; but after we have done all, we must always end with this,—that the uttermost is just the uttermost; and beyond the uttermost, neither the experience of man can pass, nor the imagination of man can picture.

Now, as there is something that is the very uttermost in the world of time, and as there is something that is the very uttermost in the world of space, so there is something that is the very uttermost in the world of sin and in the world of salvation. It is not given to any mortal man to know when the uttermost moment of time is to come. " Of that day, and that hour, knoweth no man : no, not the angels which are in heaven : neither the Son, but the Father." And as for the uttermost point of space, some men of science are so perplexed with it as to think that space must be absolutely infinite, like its Maker.

And no more does any man know what is the uttermost limit of sin and misery. Who is the uttermost of all sinners ?—who can tell ? But that there is such a sinner somewhere, still sinning on earth, or saved in heaven, or suffering in hell ; and that Almighty God knows that sinner, and knows all about him,—all that is quite certain. There is something in that sinner's case, there has been something in that sinner's career, that conclusively stamps him as the very uttermost of all sinners anywhere to be found. In God's sight, and in God's judgment, there is some sinner somewhere, who bears away the palm.

" All have sinned and come short of the glory of God." But there are great differences in the length to which sinners have gone in their sins. " All sins are in all," said the Stoics ; " but all sins have not come to the light in all." There is no sin so sinful but that any sinner might have committed it. At the same time, and as a matter

16

of fact, some sinners far outstrip other sinners, and leave them quite out of sight. " Are all transgressions of the law equally heinous ? " No. By no means. " Some sins in themselves, and by reason of several aggravations, are more heinous in the sight of God than others." Now, it is the " aggravations " of our sins that carry us away past all other sinners, and make us the very uttermost of all sinners. And thus it is that the uttermost sinner is not at all to be looked for where we would first think of looking for him. We speak of Christendom, and of heathendom. And we would naturally look for the chief of sinners among the nations that know not God. But he is not to be found where we would naturally look for him. Not at all. " Circumstances," says a great experimental preacher, " lie far heavier on the soul than the sin itself." And the circumstances of a sinner in a Christian land lie far heavier on his conscience, and stand far blacker against him in the book of judgment, than if he had lived and died in a heathen land. This is how a deeply exercised saint used to examine himself as to the circumstances and the aggravations of his sins. " My age," he used to say, " and my office ? My place of love, and honour, and trust, in the family, and in the Church ? The time and the occasion of my sin ? The true name of my sin, if it were to be proclaimed from the housetop ? The contempt and the defiance of

God revealed in my sin ? Done once only ? or
done often ? and done presumptuously, and done
insultingly, and after frequent forgiveness ? " And
so on, through a whole world of circumstances and
aggravations. Yes; it is the circumstances and
the accompaniments of sin that so blacken the
book of God, and so exasperate and horrify the
awakened conscience of the sinner.

And thus it is that the very uttermost sinner in
all this city this morning is to be looked for in some
of its congregations, rather than in any of its slums
or in any of its prisons. Those outcast creatures
that fill our sunken places, our prisons, and our
penal settlements, may well have committed
crimes that we have never had any temptation to
commit. But by no possibility can they be guilty
of such sins, and such heinous aggravations of sins,
as some of us are guilty of. They never had the
thousandth part of our advantages and oppor-
tunities. And it is advantage and opportunity
that so aggravate sin, and so incriminate the soul.
I should not wonder then that the very uttermost
sinner in all this city this morning is sitting in this
house at this moment, and is consenting to my
words about him with his whole heart. It is quite
possible, and there are some good grounds for
believing it, that there is some man here on whom
privilege upon privilege has been heaped, and
opportunity upon opportunity, and grace upon

grace, and all conceivable kinds of blessing—both
temporal and spiritual—and yet he has sinned in
the teeth of all that till he is the very uttermost
sinner in all this city.   And till it may very well be
that what is so much mere hypothesis, and imagination, and indeed extravagance, to all other
men now listening to his case, is the most un-
deniable truth, and the most dreadful truth to him.
Ay—and it may very well be that, under the hand
of the Holy Ghost, he may be seeing at this moment
how near he now is to the last precipice of all,
how near he now is to that black line of reproba-
tion beyond which there is nothing but the bottom-
less pit.   But he is still here.   He has not yet
crossed the black line.   He has not yet fallen head-
long into that horrible pit.   " Save from going
down to the pit !   For I have found a ransom."
" Bring forth the best robe, and put it on him.
For this my son was dead, and is alive again ; he
was lost, and is found ! "

But that is not all.   Would God it were all.   But
it is not all, by a long way.   For, over and above
the outward world of actual and aggravated sin,
there is the far more awful world of secret sinfulness, a whole world of inward wickedness that far
surpasses all our powers of self-examination.   And
here also, there must be some saint of God, somewhere,—either in grace or in glory, either on earth
or in heaven,—who had, or who has, in himself,

the very uttermost of "indwelling sin." Who, I
wonder, was he ? Or, if he is now alive, who is he ?
Was it David who was wont to cry that there was
"no rest in his bones because of his sin " ? And
again, that his "loins were filled with a loathsome
disease " ? And again, that he was "shapen in
iniquity " ? Or was it Isaiah ? "Woe is me, for
I am undone ! " Or was it Daniel when his
"comeliness was turned to corruption " ? Or was
it the Apostle Paul, whose seventh chapter is such an
outburst of unparalleled agony ? Or was it Luther ?
"When a man like me," says the Reformer, "comes
to know the plague of his own heart, he is not
miserable only, he is absolute misery itself." Or
was it Samuel Rutherford, who used to say :
"When I look at the sinfulness of my own heart,
my salvation is to me my Saviour's greatest miracle.
He has accomplished nothing like my salvation " ?
Or was it Jacob Behmen, the uttermost of God's
unsanctified saints, when he wrote : "Do not mis-
take me, for my heart is as full of malice sometimes
as it can hold " ? "Begone ! " shouted Philip Neri
to those who spoke to his praise—"Begone ! for I
am good for nothing but to think and to do evil ! "
"I am made of sin," sobbed Bishop Andrewes, till
his private prayer-book was all but undecipherable
to his literary executors because of its author's
sweat and tears. "It has often appeared to me,"
said the seraphic Jonathan Edwards, "that if God

were to mark my heart iniquity against me, my bed would be in hell." But time would fail me to tell you the half of the agonising cries that I hear going up to heaven from the utmost corner of the land.

Now, which of all these was the "uttermost" sufferer because of his indwelling sin—who shall say ?—or whether it was any of those sufferers, or whether that greatest sufferer may not be some one of ourselves. Who can tell ? It is quite possible ; and the day will declare. For " the secret of the Lord is with them that fear Him ; and He will show them His holy covenant."

We cannot be absolutely sure till we see them with our own eyes in heaven ; but I think I am quite safe in saying that their Saviour has saved all those great sinners by this time, and that to " the utter-most." He has saved them from the uttermost of actual sin, and of indwelling sinfulness, and to the uttermost of holiness and of blessedness. I say, " the uttermost of holiness and of blessedness." For it is only those who have known in themselves the very " uttermost " of actual and indwelling sin, and all the shame and all the pain of it, who can by any possibility attain to the " uttermost " possession and enjoyment of true holiness, and the full blessedness of heaven. And there is a real fitness and fairness in that. " Blessed are they which do hunger and thirst after righteousness : for they shall be filled." And again : " Him that overcometh will I make a pillar in the temple of My God, and he shall go no more out. And I will write upon him the name of My God, and the name of the city of My God ; and I will write upon him My new name."

The builder of a temple, who spares no expense, will sometimes bring his pillars from the very ends of the earth. Wherever he hears of a rock with rich enough veins of colour in it, and which is, at the same time, capable of taking on the finest finish, which is able to bear all his carving-tools, and to receive all his intended polish and resplendence— at any cost, he will bring home such stones, and will with them rear a long vista of such pillars ; till his temple is a perfect vision and a praise of all kinds of beauty. And something like that, says " He that is holy, He that is true," will it be in the heavenly temple. It is not by any means any and every stone that will take on all that is in the Master-Builder's mind. It is not every pillar that will carry all His Father's name, and all His own new name. And thus it is that wherever the Heavenly Builder finds such a possible " pillar," even if it is in the " utmost corner of the land," at any price He will purchase it for His great design, and will not leave off working on it, till He has set it, and in its proper place, in His heavenly temple.

And then, when, at the end of this world, that heavenly temple is at last finished—what a vision of strength and of beauty it will be! And supported and adorned with what a forest of dear-bought and far-borne pillars! And every pillar of them all written all over with the Builder's new name, and with His Father's name.

But, "What is His name, and what is His Son's name?" if thou canst tell. Yes, I can tell, and I will tell you. For, when a Gospel preacher is in the Spirit on the Lord's Day, a door is opened to him in heaven, and he is carried up to see the temple of God, and all its pillars, till he is able to tell, to all who have ears to hear, what is to be written on all the living pillars of that living temple. "Merciful," will be one of God's names written in letters of gold on many pillars. "Gracious," in like letters on many other pillars. "Long-suffering," upon some; and "abundant in goodness and in truth," upon some. "He brought me up also out of an horrible pit, out of the miry clay," will shine on one great pillar; and on another, "Out of the belly of hell cried I, and He heard my voice." And on a pillar of the rarest beauty and perfection of form, this: "O wretched man that I was! But I thank God through Jesus Christ my Lord." Now what will be written upon you? What shall we gather round you and read, written upon you? For my part—you will read all these Scriptures written in large letters upon me. All these, and many more names of my God than all these. But especially,

my text of this morning will be written upon me—
" Saved to the uttermost ! " Saved to the utter-
most ! And to go no more out ! The Chief of
Sinners, and saved to the uttermost.

" Now unto Him that is able to do exceeding
abundantly above all that we ask or think, according to the power that worketh in us : unto Him be
glory in the Church by Christ Jesus throughout all
ages, world without end. Amen."

6

THE NEW WINE OF THE KINGDOM

"I say unto you, I will not drink henceforth of this fruit of the vine, until that day when I drink it new with you in My Father's kingdom."—MATT. xxvi. 29.

MILTON makes the angel say to Adam :

> " What if earth
> Be but the shadow of heaven ; and things therein
> Each to other like, more than on earth is thought ? "

That is to say : as the Passover Supper in Israel was but the " shadow " of the Lord's Supper in New Testament times, even so the Lord's Supper itself is but the " shadow " of the Marriage Supper of the Lamb. Butler also says, in his own deep and suggestive way, that " we are at present in the middle of a great progressive scheme of things : in the everlasting issues of which we are concerned far beyond all conception of ours." That is to say : the Lord's Supper is but one step in a great progressive scheme of evangelical things : of which we, at present, see next to nothing of their perfected end. And thus it is that this text, as it falls from our Lord's lips, carries the Lord's Supper away

out of this present world of things altogether, and
carries it away up into the new heavens and the
new earth. The Lord's Supper, as we now celebrate
it, has a great historical and commemorative signi-
ficance. But it has a great prophetic and anticipa-
tive aspect also, in that it so plainly, and so
impressively, points forward to the Marriage Supper
of the Lamb. Let us take the Lord's Supper, then,
as it is spread before us this morning, as the earthly
" shadow " of the heavenly Supper : let us look
on our greatest means of grace on earth as, after
all, but the sacramental pledge and foretaste of
the far better things that God is preparing for them
that love Him.

To begin at the beginning : What was Moses, and
his paschal lamb, but the " shadow," not so much of
the Lord's Supper on earth as of His far better
Supper in heaven ? The Old Testament lamb of
Moses was the type of the New Testament Lamb of
God. But for the once that our sin-atoning Lord
is called " The Lamb of God " in the Gospel, He is
called by that same atonement-Name, actually,
twenty-nine times in the Revelation. Now this
continual remembrance of that atonement-Name
of His in heaven is not without a great lesson to us
—surely. That continually recurring Name of His
in heaven is surely intended to teach us that we
shall see " the Lamb of God " in heaven, " as He
was slain " on earth; and that we shall see Him

then, with far more wonder, and far more praise than we can possibly see Him now. So true is it, and so true will it then be seen to be that this earth, at its best, is " but the shadow of heaven; and things therein each to other like, more than on earth is thought."

But to come down to our own day. Did you ever think, as you enjoyed them beyond all words, that all our Communion Seasons on earth are but so many shadows of the innumerable Communion Seasons that will come round to us in heaven ? Sweet and sanctifying as they are, our very best Communion Seasons are not yet the Marriage Supper of the Lamb. At their best, our returning Communion Seasons are but the Betrothal Suppers of the Lamb. But in His Father's house in heaven, there will be a real and a true Marriage Supper ; when our too-long betrothal will, at last, be " fulfilled,"—to use the Bridegroom's own glad word about it. Yes ; and as those Communion Seasons, so to call them, come round in that world of things where time shall be no longer, but where there shall be something in the place of time—something that it hath not entered into the mind of man to imagine in the revolving years, so to call them, of the life everlasting,—there will, no doubt, be seasons when all our past, both on earth and in heaven, will be called to remembrance, and will be sealed down anew upon our souls. And as we have " silver

weddings " and " golden weddings " and " diamond
weddings " on earth, in which we joyfully com-
memorate our happiest and our longest-lived
weddings, even so there will be days of silver, and
days of gold, and days of diamond in heaven, on
which all the electing love of the Father, and all the
redeeming love of the Son, and all the indwelling
love of the Holy Ghost, will, again and again, be
commemorated; and that in a way far more than
a merely sacramental way.   For, then, a far

> " . . . higher gift than grace
> Shall flesh and blood refine :
> Christ's Presence, and His very Self,
> And Essence all-Divine."

And then, for my part—do not be afraid or
offended—I fully expect to enjoy not Communion
Sabbaths only in heaven, but Fast Days as well.
Not Fast Days, indeed, when we shall hang our
heads like a bulrush, and spread sackcloth and ashes
under us.   But Fast Days—so to call them—that
shall be wholly fit for heaven, and entirely appro-
priate to heaven.   We shall not indeed " examine
ourselves " in heaven, as to our broken vows since
last communion.   But we shall sit apart for a
season, watching with our Lord for " one hour,"
and shall examine ourselves as to our growth in
glory, and in our ever-increasing likeness to Christ.
There will be days in which we shall ask ourselves
as to whether we are keeping sufficiently in mind

the hole of the pit out of which we were dug. As also, if we are continually recollecting all else that God, in Christ, has done for our souls. And I quite anticipate that, at such seasons of self-examination, there will be some among us who will have a certain sadness in our souls, as we call to mind the communion seasons of earth; and recollect how little we really examined and condemned ourselves on our appointed days of repentance, and with how little true preparation we ventured unto the Table. And all that will make us hasten to put on again the Wedding Garment of our Lord's imputed righteousness, clothed and adorned with which we shall again sit down at His Table, and with this never-to-be-forgotten Psalm in our mouth:

> " With us He dealt not as we sinned,
> Nor did requite our ill."

" Where wilt Thou," said Peter and John, " that we prepare for Thee to eat the Passover ? " And He said unto them: " Behold, when ye have entered into the city, ye shall find a large upper room furnished: there make ready." And the two disciples did as they were commanded. And they took the blood of the paschal lamb in a basin, and they struck it on the two side-posts, and on the upper doorpost of the house in which they were to eat the Passover. And the blood was a token upon that house all that night, until the morning.

Peter and John were, in that way, our Lord's fore-runners that Passover night in Jerusalem. But our Lord is our Forerunner Himself in preparing for us to eat our true Passover Supper in the New Jerusalem. Indeed, our Lord bears in heaven that very Name. "The Forerunner," says the Apostle, "even Jesus, is for us entered. By His own blood He hath for us entered into the Holy Place "— even as He said : " I go to prepare a place for you." "Now," says an old preacher on this point, "a forerunner is always a forerunner of followers; and of such followers as stay not long behind. And our Lord bears that excellent Name because He has gone on before us to take up a place for us in His Father's House of many mansions. Earthly forerunners," that old preacher proceeds, " are wont to write the names of those who are to follow them, sometimes with chalk, and sometimes with paint, on the doors of the allotted lodgings ; but we have such a ' Forerunner ' that He writes our names on the doorposts of heaven with His own blood. The sprinkled blood of the paschal lamb signed and sealed the identity and the ownership and the safety of every true Israelite's house in the land of Egypt. But all that was only an earthly ' shadow ' of our far better signed and sealed lintel and doorpost in the new heaven and the new earth."

"And Jesus took bread, and blessed it, and

brake it, and gave it to His disciples, and said to
them: Take, eat: this is My Body broken for you.
And He took the cup, and gave thanks, and gave
it to them, saying: Drink ye all of it." The
Reformed Church finds two sacraments in Holy
Scripture; while the Church of Rome finds seven
in the Scriptures and in Church-tradition. But
the Church of Christ in Glory will have a whole
multitude of sacraments. Indeed, there will be
nothing to be seen, or tasted, or touched in heaven
that will not be a true and a fruitful sacrament.

For,—"What is a Sacrament?" "A Sacrament is an holy ordinance instituted by Christ,
wherein, by sensible signs, Christ and the benefits
of the New Covenant are represented, sealed, and
applied to believers." And the whole of our
Father's House, and of our own mansions in our
Father's House, will be as full as they can hold of
such sensible signs: so far as our senses will hold
there, and will have their objects there. In this
respect, it will be with us in heaven, as it was with
our Lord on earth. Everything He saw, as He
went about, was a sacrament to Him. That is to
say,—everything He saw around Him represented,
and sealed, and applied the New Covenant and all
its benefits, to Him and to His disciples. Did He,
in one of His walks abroad, see a husbandman
sowing seed in his field? So is the Kingdom of
heaven, He said to Himself, and to His disciples.

Did He see a vineyard, or a barren fig tree, or a lost sheep, or a piece of leaven, or a marriage supper, or a friend out at midnight to borrow loaves ? —absolutely everything that our Lord saw on earth, in one way or other, spoke to Him something more concerning the Kingdom of heaven. And the same sacramental,—that is to say, the same spiritual and imaginative mind, will by that time be found in all of us who shall be counted worthy communicants at the Table above. " Praise Him," we shall all sing with the Psalmist. " Praise Him, all ye His angels : praise Him, all ye His hosts. Praise Him, sun and moon ; and all ye stars of light . . . mountains, and all hills : fruitful trees, and all cedars : beasts, and all cattle : creeping things, and flying fowl . . . both young men, and maidens : old men, and children. . . . Praise Him with the sound of the trumpet. Praise Him with the psaltery and the harp. Praise Him with the timbrel, and in the dance. Praise Him with stringed instruments, and with organs. Yea : let everything that hath breath all unite to praise the Lord." So sacramental will the whole of creation have become to us all by that time. But most of all, the glorified Soul, and the glorified Body of our Redeemer, with the sacramental marks of our redemption remaining on His hands, and on His feet, and on His side. " It was a wise design of Mark Antony," says Jeremy Taylor, " when he

17

would stir up the people to revenge the death of
Cæsar: he brought the dead body to the pleading-
place, and showed to all men his deadly wounds.
He held up Cæsar's stabbed mantle: the very
mantle he put on that night in which he beat the
Nervii. He put his finger in that fatal wound
through which the dagger had pierced Cæsar's
heart. And he told them with what a love that
heart had always loved them: so much so, that he
had made the people of Rome the heirs of all his
glory, and all his wealth; and had left to them so
many places of delight and pleasure. And then,
it was but natural that their grief at the loss of
so honourable and so loved a lord should fill the
people with a great sorrow, and a great revenge."

And in like manner, there will be pleading-days
and pleading-places in heaven where we shall see
the "Lamb as He had been slain"; and where we
shall be filled, as never before, with a great sorrow,
and a great revenge, and an ever greater love. Yea,
with what indignation; yea, with what fear; yea,
with what vehement desire; yea, with what zeal;
yea, with what revenge, shall all our hearts be filled
full! Till our full hearts shall again find vent in
this commemoration psalm:

"Unto Him that loved us, and washed us from
all our sins in His own blood; to Him be glory and
dominion and power, for ever and ever. Amen!"

"But I say unto you, I will not henceforth drink

of this fruit of the vine, until that day when I shall
drink it new with you in My Father's Kingdom."
I will drink wine new with you. That is to say—
wine of a new kind. Wine out of a new vineyard.
Wine out of a new winepress. Wine of a new
sweetness, and a new strength, and a new exhilaration. The fruit of the True Vine is love, joy, peace,
gentleness, and all kinds of goodness; but, especially,
love.

" Thy love is better than wine," the Bride shall
say to the Bridegroom, as she leans on His breast
at their Marriage Supper. And the Bridegroom
shall answer her : " I am come into my garden, my
sister, my spouse : I have gathered my myrrh
with my spice : I have drunk my wine with my
milk : eat, O Friends : drink, yea, drink abundantly,
O Beloved." " This is my Beloved," shall the
Bride then boast to all the daughters of Jerusalem.
" This is my Beloved, and this is my Friend ! "
For I am my Beloved's : and He is mine ! Yea,
I am His, and He is mine !

Yes !—O Angel !

" What if earth
Be but the shadow of heaven ; and things therein
Each to other like, more than on earth is thought ! "

LAST MESSAGES

7

A STUDY IN THE SWELLING OF JORDAN

" How wilt thou do in the swelling of Jordan ? "—JER. xii. 5.

BOTH in its disputed rise, and in its zigzag course, and then in its inscrutable fall—the Jordan is the most wonderful, and indeed, in some respects, the most mysterious river on the face of the earth. Rising among the obscure rocks and tangled forests of the Lebanon, the Jordan rushes down through a deep and a tortuous gorge, that has seldom seen a bridge, and that only here and there has admitted a ford for the foot of man or beast. Walled in by high and overhanging rocks, the Jordan runs its crooked and angry course for some 200 miles, till it loses itself in the Salt Sea, the Dead Sea of Sodom and Gomorrah. It was the absolutely miraculous passage of the Jordan by Joshua and the priests and the people of Israel, that gave the Jordan such a place of wonder and of praise in the prophets and psalmists of Israel. And as time went on, the passage of the Jordan became a proverb and a prophecy of the passing of the immortal soul, out of this life of bitter bondage and of long and sore pilgrimage, into the Promised Land, the Promised Land of our Heavenly Father's House. And then, the prophet's solemnising challenge— "*How wilt thou do in the swelling of Jordan?*"—that has come powerfully home to every man who has an evil conscience, and who has it before him to die and to go to judgment.

Well, then, before we come to *ourselves*, let us take a few moments to look at how some of our forerunners did when *they* came to the swelling of *their* " Jordan." And, first—let us look at our blessed Lord Himself, when He was approaching the dark river of death. For though He had no sin of His own to burden His conscience and to darken His heart, yet, at the same time, He was made such a surety and such a substitute for sinners that the swelling of His Jordan became an agony ; and indeed, a terror to Him—so much so, that even the pen of inspiration trembles to describe His dying experiences. Listen, then, with all the holy fear you can command, to what is tremblingly written concerning even the " Jordan " of our sinless Lord. " Now is My soul troubled ; and what shall I say ? Father, save Me from this hour." " Then took He with Him Peter and the two sons of Zebedee, and began to be sorrowful, and very heavy. Then saith He unto them, ' My soul is exceeding sorrowful, even unto death : tarry ye here, and watch with

Me.' And then He went a little farther, and fell on His face, and prayed, saying : ' O My Father, if it be possible, let this cup pass from Me : nevertheless not as I will, but as Thou wilt.' " As Mark has it : " He began to be sore amazed, and to be very heavy." And as Luke has it : " Being in an agony, He prayed more earnestly : and His sweat was as it were great drops of blood falling to the ground. And on the morrow, when it was about the sixth hour, there was a great darkness over all the land until the ninth hour. And the sun was darkened ; and the veil of the temple was rent in the midst. And, when He had received the vinegar, Jesus cried with a loud voice and said, ' Father ! into Thy hands I commend My spirit ! ' And, having said this, He gave up the ghost." Now that, my brethren, was somewhat of how our Lord did in the swelling of *His* Jordan.

" And one of the malefactors which were crucified beside Him railed on Him, and said, ' If Thou be Christ, save Thyself and us.' But the other answering rebuked him, saying, ' Dost thou not fear God, seeing thou art in the same condemnation ? And we indeed justly ; for we receive the due reward of our deeds : but this man hath done nothing amiss.' And he said unto Jesus, ' Lord, remember me when Thou comest into Thy Kingdom.' And Jesus said to him, ' Verily I say unto thee, To-day thou shalt be with Me in Paradise.' " And *that* was how the penitent thief did in the swelling of *his* Jordan.

And *this* is how Stephen, the martyr-deacon, did. After he had spoken his great speech, his enemies were cut to the heart, and they rose upon him with one accord, and cast him out of the city, and stoned him to death ; and he died calling upon God, and saying : "Lord Jesus, receive my spirit, and lay not this sin to their charge." And they laid down their clothes at a young man's feet, whose name was Saul. And thirty years after that, Saul, by that time called Paul, descended into *his* Jordan with these words : "I thank Christ Jesus our Lord for putting me into the ministry : me, who was before a blasphemer and a persecutor : but I obtained mercy ; that in me Jesus Christ might show forth all His long-suffering for a pattern to them which should hereafter believe on Him to life everlasting. And now, I am ready to be offered, and the time of my departure is at hand. And henceforth there is laid up for me a crown of righteousness, which the Lord, the righteous Judge, shall give me at that day ; and not to me only, but unto all them also that love His appearing."

When Augustine saw that the swelling of *his* Jordan was fast approaching him, he got one of his divinity students to paint the thirty-second Psalm on the wall opposite his bed. And that great

saint descended into his dark river, singing and
saying :

> " O blessed is the man to whom
>   Is freely pardonèd
> All the transgression he hath done,
>   Whose sin is coverèd.
> I will confess unto the Lord
>   My trespasses, said I ;
> And of my sin Thou freely didst
>   Forgive the iniquity."

" Venerable Father," said Justus Jonas to
Luther, when *he* was nearing *his* dark river :
" Venerable Father, do you die trusting in Jesus
Christ as your God and Saviour, and subscribing
to the whole reformed doctrines that you con-
stantly preached to us ? "   " Yes, certainly ! "
shouted the great Reformer with his last breath.
" Yes, certainly !   Jesus Christ is my Lord and my
God, and He is my alone Righteousness and Strength
both in death as in life ! "

But by far and away our best handbook and
guide-book as we draw near the swelling of *our*
Jordan is John Bunyan's marvellous narrative of
the various experiences of his puritan pilgrims, as
they approached the dark river, and went through
it.   " Now, I further saw that betwixt them and
the gate above there was a River ; but there was
no bridge over the River ; and the River was very
deep.   Then they addressed themselves to the
water ; and, entering, Christian began to sink, till

he cried out to Hopeful, his neighbour, ' I sink in deep waters, the billows go over my head : all His angry waves go over me.' But Hopeful said, ' Be of good cheer, my Brother, for I feel the bottom ; and it is good.' And with that Christian broke out with a loud voice, ' O ! I see Him again ! and He says to me, When thou passest through the waters, I will be with thee : and through the rivers, they shall not overflow thee.' "

And some time afterwards, when Christiana, the widow of Christian the pilgrim, came within sight of the same river, she called for Mr. Greatheart, her guide, and told him how matters stood with her. So he answered her, that he was heartily glad for her sake, and that he could have been glad had the heavenly post come for him. Then she called for her children ; and what she said to them is all to be read at the end of her fine history. The last words she was heard to say here, were these : " I come, Lord, to be with Thee, and to bless Thee."

The next of that pilgrim company to come to the River was Mr. Ready-to-halt. And the last words he was heard to say were these : " Welcome life." So he also went on his way.

After this, the same post sounded his horn at the chamber door of Mr. Feeble-Mind. And his last words were : " Hold out, Faith and Patience ! " And saying so, he also went over to the other side.

How Mr Despondency and his daughter Miss

Much-Afraid got over, and what they said, I leave
you to read for your own desponding and much-
afraid selves.

As, also, dear old Honest, and his last words.
And Mr. Valiant-for-Truth, and his brave words
about his sword, and about his marks and his scars
that he carried over with him. And to crown all
—the magnificent speech of Mr. Standfast. Than
which, even John Bunyan never penned two nobler
pages. But how glorious it was to see how the
regions beyond the dark River were all filled with
horses and chariots; with pipers and with
trumpeters; with singers with the voice and with
players on stringed instruments; and all to welcome the pilgrims as they went up and followed
one another in at the Beautiful Gate of the City!
But among all John Bunyan's characters and
their end, do not forget Mr. Fearing, who is in
some respects the Tinker's spiritual and literary
masterpiece.

And now, after all that, I will only take time to
give you Bishop Butler and *his* Jordan. When
the great moralist, the old Honest of the Episcopal
Bench, was on his death-bed, he called for his
chaplain, and said to him: " Though I have en-
deavoured to avoid sin, and to please God to the
utmost of my power; yet from the consciousness
of perpetual infirmities, I am still afraid to die."
" My lord," said the chaplain, " you have for-

gotten that Jesus Christ is a Saviour." "True," said Butler; "but how shall I know that He is a Saviour for *me*?" "My lord, it is written, Him that cometh unto Me, I will in no wise cast out." "True," said the bishop; "and I am surprised that though I have read that Scripture a thousand times over, I never felt its virtue till this moment. And now I die happy."

Now, my brethren, let it be well understood and believed that all these dying men—from Jesus Christ Himself downward—were all but so many pioneers and forerunners to teach us how *we* are to do when we come to the swelling of our Jordan. And first, let us learn some much-needed lessons from our Lord Himself. And especially, *this* great lesson—to say at every step of our approach to our Jordan, and at every soul-sinking billow of it —"Thy will be done!" Our Lord had been saying these same sonship-words every day, and all His days; and accordingly these same sonship-words came naturally and fully and finally to His believing lips at the end of His days. For one thing, He had prayed, and that without ceasing, for thirty years, for the conversion of His un-believing brothers and sisters at home in Nazareth. And hitherto He had prayed, as it seemed, in vain. And worse, it seemed, than in vain. For, year after year, they all seemed to go farther away from their true salvation than ever before. And yet, in all that, Christ may only have been made, more and more, like to you and to me. For years, year after year, some of you may have been praying and waiting for the true conversion of some one or more dear to you ; and like your Lord, you may have to die and to leave them as they were, only worse. And *that* may well be *the* cross of all your crosses on your death-bed.

My brethren, travellers in the Holy Land tell us that the Jordan is sometimes very mysterious, very dark, very deep, very crooked, and sometimes very angry, and without a bridge to cross it or a ford to wade it. It was so to your Lord, and it is enough for this life that the disciple be as his Lord was. My brethren, if the Son of God and the Prince of believers and your great High Priest had to say, as He looked around on His unconverted family circle, " Thy will be done," it is enough for you to be able to say the same thing. But what you are never to know here of the dark mystery of your unanswered prayer, you will certainly know hereafter : even *as He now knows*.

And then, Paul's old age and the nearness of his Jordan have taught many old men, and especially many old ministers, this lesson. " I am now ready to be offered, and the time of my departure is at hand. Do thy diligence therefore to come to me shortly. And bring with thee the cloak I left at Troas, and the books, and especially the parch-

ments." And so it is with some of the successors
of the book-loving apostle. You will go into the
old-age chamber of some of your ministers and you
will find near their chair, and near their bed, such
old-age books and such Jordan-bank books as
these : John's Revelation open at the twenty-first
and twenty-second chapters ; and Dante's *Para-
diso* ; and Bunyan's *Pilgrim's Progress* ; and
Baxter's *Saints' Rest* ; and Howe's *Blessedness of
the Righteous* ; and Rutherford's *Letters* ; and New-
man's *Dream of Gerontius* ; and the *Olney* and the
Wesley Hymns. Many years ago, I went into the
death-chamber of an elder of this congregation,
and he laid his hand on the *Westminster Confession
of Faith* lying open at the great chapter on Justification ; and he said to me, " Sir, I am dying in
the strength of that peace-speaking chapter." Do
thy diligence to bring the right books, as soon as
possible, wrote Paul to Timothy, his son in the
Gospel.

And all men who are of a philosophic turn of
mind will take *their* lesson from Bishop Butler's
death-bed. " Him that cometh unto Me," said the
Saviour, " I will in no wise cast out."

> " I've read a thousand times that Scripture o'er,
>   Nor felt its truth till now I near the tomb :
>   It is enough ! O Saviour Christ, I come."

" It was Bishop Butler who made me a Christian,"
said Dr. Chalmers to his students, generously con-

fessing his indebtedness to the great philosopher. Let us all, like Dr. Chalmers, take the same philosopher for our everyday example — this day and every day—till we take him for our example on the last day of our earthly pilgrimage, and for our Jordan-side example, and say with him : " O Lamb of God, I come."

" Just as I am, without one plea
But that Thy blood was shed for me,
And that Thou bidd'st me come to Thee,
    O Lamb of God, I come.

Just as I am, and waiting not
To rid my soul of one dark blot,
To Thee, whose blood can cleanse each spot,
    O Lamb of God, I come.

Just as I am, though tossed about
With many a conflict, many a doubt,
Fightings and fears within, without,
    O Lamb of God, I come.

Just as I am, of that free love
The breadth, length, depth, and height to prove,
Here for a season, then above,
    O Lamb of God, I come." Amen.

" And then shall the King say unto them on His right hand : Come, ye blessed of My Father, inherit the Kingdom prepared for you from the foundation of the world."

And to all who so come to Him, and who keep so coming, He will surely say : " When thou passest through the waters, I will be with thee ; and through

18

the rivers, they shall not overflow thee " : " till the redeemed of the Lord shall return, and shall come to Zion with songs and with everlasting joy upon their heads: they shall obtain joy and gladness, and sorrow and sighing shall flee away."

8

THE HEBREW CHILD'S QUESTION AT
THE PASSOVER SUPPER

" It shall come to pass, when your children shall say unto you,
What mean ye by this service ? that ye shall say, It is the
sacrifice of the Lord's passover."—Ex. xii. 26, 27.

HAD you been a sojourner in any Hebrew house,
on any Passover night in Old Testament times,
you would have seen and heard all this. You
would have seen the head of the house killing a
lamb, and sprinkling its blood on the doorpost of
the house. The flesh of the lamb was then roasted,
and was eaten along with unleavened bread and
bitter herbs. And all the assembled family ate
their Passover supper standing on their feet, with
their loins girt and with their staff in their hand ;
and all that in haste, as if they were all ready for a
midnight escape.

And always, at this point of the ordinance, the
eldest son of the house came forward, and said to his
father : " What mean ye by this service ? " And
the head of the house always gave the same pre-
scribed reply : " This is the sacrifice of the Lord's

Passover, who *passed over* the houses of our fathers in Egypt, when He smote the Egyptians, and delivered His covenanted people." And once every year, all down the generations, the same scene was enacted : till we see, now, the child David ; and now, the child Solomon ; and now, the child Isaiah ; and now, the child Daniel; and now, the child, Jesus of Nazareth ; and now, the child Saul of Tarsus—all asking the same question, and all receiving the same answer.

Now, it cannot fail to be both interesting and instructive to us this morning, if we follow the example of the Hebrew households, and bring forward, now a young communicant, and now a foreign student, to ask what is our Lord's meaning, and what is our meaning in this and in that part of our Communion service. For there will be young communicants here this morning, whose hunger for yet fuller teaching has only been whetted by what they have been taught at home, and in the Communion class. Like the Child Jesus, Who, just because He had asked the question of the text, and had received the answer of the text, every Passover night in Nazareth, was only all the more found in the Temple at His first Passover in Jerusalem, sitting in the midst of the doctors both hearing them and asking them questions. Or again, there will be some divinity student here, from Africa or from India, or from China or from Japan, who is

seeing for the first time the Lord's Supper dispensed
in all its fulness, and in all its orderliness : and
who, student-like, is not willing to let any part of
the service pass, till he has fully and clearly understood the whole Communion ordinance as it is observed in the long evangelised and long covenanted
land of Scotland.

Now, that being so, I can imagine a young communicant coming forward at the opening of the
service this morning, and saying that he thinks he
understands why this ordinance is called sometimes
" The New Testament Passover," and sometimes
" The Lord's Supper," and sometimes " The Communion." But he was reading an English Church
Catechism the other evening, when he came on
another name that he is not sure he fully understands. And that somewhat difficult Episcopal
name is the " Eucharist." Well, that is a quite
fit and proper question to ask. And this is my
answer to that question. *Eucharist* is an un-
translated Greek work, which means *the giving of
thanks*. And you will remember how the Gospels
tell us again and again that our Lord began the
Paschal Supper that night by giving thanks to His
Father in heaven. We read that fact again and
again. But it is not so easily understood just why
He gave thanks for the bread and for the wine, and
for all that the broken bread and the poured out
wine symbolised that New Testament Passover

night. I can quite easily understand Peter and James and John giving great thanks for the Lord's Table, because they were great sinners. But that was just what their Master was not. " He knew no sin " ; and therefore He did not need the redemption from sin that was set forth by that broken bread and that poured out wine. For what then did He give thanks ? For what, communicants, but for this, that it is far more blessed to give redemption than it is to receive it ; and it was for that supreme blessedness of His, that night, that He gave His Father such heartfelt thanks. Old William Grant of Ayr has answered your difficulty about Christ's Passover thanks, in these true and beautiful Communion lines of his :

> " And could'st Thou, Lord, Thy thanks express
> In prospect of Thy deep distress ?
> And at the Table, spread to show
> Thy symbols of Thy coming woe.
>
> And could'st Thou bless Thy God on high,
> That He had sent Thee thus to die,
> And for our sins to give Thee up
> To drink wrath's overwhelming cup ?
>
> O ! what a love must Thine have been !
> To *praise* in view of such a scene !
> When broken bread, and poured out wine,
> Portrayed those bitter woes of Thine."

Yes ; I think my dear old friend has here given the true reply to your question about the Eucharist :

that is to say, about our Saviour's giving of thanks at the table that night.

Again, you will all have observed that the first thing the officiating minister does at the head of the Table is to read what he calls the "warrant" for what he and the elders and the communicants are about to do. Now, what is a "warrant"? What is it but a permission, a sanction, a legalisation of something that is about to be done? But we take our place at the Lord's Table to-day on far stronger grounds than any mere warrant. For we came to His Table at our Lord's express desire and earnest wish: nay, we come at His express command. "Do this," He says, "in remembrance of Me." "Take, eat," He says, handing round the bread; "this is My body broken for you: this do in remembrance of Me." And, "This cup is the New Testament in My blood, therefore, this also do ye in remembrance of Me." "For," adds the apostle, "as often as ye eat this bread and drink this cup, ye do show forth the Lord's death till He come." So that, you see, we will neglect the Lord's Table at our peril: yes, at our peril: as we shall answer to Him, at His coming, for having boldly disobeyed His dying command, and for openly despising and trampling upon His body and His blood.

But then, on the other hand, there is what is called "fencing the Table." Now you all know at once what a fence is—for what purpose a shepherd runs a fence round his sheepfold. Well: all men, the very worst, are welcome; and at all times are welcome to the Saviour. There are no fences run around the Cross. But, in the nature of things, all men are not welcome, as yet, to the Lord's Table. Why—the very apostle of free grace, of full and immediate and abounding grace to all men, spends the half of his First Epistle to the sanctified in Corinth, in running a strong and a sharp fence round the Lord's Table in that so corrupt city. And then, not apostles and pastors only are on occasion to fence the Lord's Table; but there are times and circumstances when intending communicants themselves are rigidly to fence themselves away from the Table. For, " it is required of them that would worthily partake of the Lord's Supper, that they examine themselves of their knowledge to discern the Lord's body, of their faith to feed upon Him, of their repentance, love, and new obedience : lest, coming unworthily, they eat and drink judgment to themselves." But then, truly and properly speaking, no man is, or ever will be, worthy to partake of the Table of the Lord. But worthiness is one thing, when a communicant is looked at as he is in himself; and it is quite another thing, when he is looked at as in Christ, and as invited and indeed commanded by Christ to come to His Table.

> " I am not worthy ; cold and bare
>   The lodging of my soul ;
> How canst Thou deign to enter there ?
>   Lord, speak, and make me whole.
>
> O come, in this sweet morning hour
>   Feed me with food divine ;
> And fill with all Thy love and power
>   This worthless heart of mine."

At this stage of our service, a divinity student, say from India, comes forward, and says that, though he had often heard the Scottish missionaries speak of the *Shorter Catechism* with profound reverence, he had never had the least idea of the intellectual power and the spiritual depth of that scriptural document, till he came to the New College and commenced to study divinity seriously, seriously and with all his might. And just last night when he was working his way through the sacramental chapters of the Catechism to prepare himself for this morning, he came on the passage that promised him " spiritual nourishment "— spiritual nourishment and growth in grace—at the Table to-day. And he would like to learn more of what the Catechism means by " spiritual nourishment and growth in grace." Well, the answer is this : The communicant's body is not nourished at the Lord's Table : it is his soul ; it is his spirit that is nourished here. " Let every man eat his own supper at home, for his bodily nourishment," says the Apostle. But he who would have his soul and spirit nourished to more and more spiritual and eternal life, let him come, by faith, to the Lord's Table. As Robert Bruce (that stately Presbyterian divine, as David Masson calls him) said in his Fourth Sermon on the Sacraments, delivered in the High Kirk of Edinburgh in the year 1590: "The flesh of Christ is not like any other eaten flesh: the flesh of Christ is such that it is really not my bodily but my spiritual nourishment. The flesh of Christ symbolised by the broken bread serves me to my spiritual life; and for this reason, it is called my spiritual food. It is called spiritual in respect of the end and design for which I partake of it; because when I, by faith, aright partake of it, I am thereby nourished not to a bodily life but to a spiritual and a heavenly life." Let every true student of the Sacraments read Robert Bruce in his so racy Scotch; and along with Bruce, Jonathan Edwards on the *Religious Affections*. Two masterly men to be read and read again by all true students of these divine matters. For my part, I read them both every pre-communion week.

Another thing that will have arrested the young communicants last week, as they read the history of the Lord's Supper as it was instituted that Passover night, was this: "A new commandment," said Christ to His disciples, "I give unto you at My Table: and that is that ever after this night

you shall love one another, as I have loved you."
A *new commandment*, He said, and with a great
emphasis. And yet all the time that was an old
commandment. That was a commandment as old
as when man was first made in the image of the
God of love. But all old things were made new
that great new-creation night, in the upper room.
And that new commandment of brotherly love
must have come home with new and poignant
power even to the dullest mind and the hardest
heart at that New Testament Table. For it was
only yesterday that they had all scandalised their
Master, by the way they had " disputed " as they
came up to Jerusalem to the Passover ; disputed
with a great heat as to who would be greatest in
the coming Kingdom. And it was in His great
shame and pain at their envious and angry quarrel,
that their Master poured water into a basin, and
took a towel and washed their feet : as also, put
into the hands of every one of them, Judas Iscariot
and all, the broken bread and the poured out wine
of His body and His blood. " As I have loved
you, that ye go and love and serve one another,"
He said : " rejoicing in one another's greatness in
My Kingdom, more than in your own greatness
therein." Yes ; a new commandment, because
issued on such a new ground that Lord's Supper
night.

During the dispensation of the Lord's Supper

that night, six of the twelve disciples came forward
and put Passover questions to their Master.   Judas
and Peter and John, and Thomas and Philip and
Judas, not Iscariot—all put Passover questions to
Him ; and we have the answers that they all got.
But there was one thing that our Lord said and
did that night, concerning which no one seems to
have felt any difficulty, or started any inquiry.
" Verily," He said, " I will drink no more of the
fruit of the vine, till I drink it new with you in the
Kingdom of God."   What did He mean ?   What
exactly did He mean them and us to understand
by that mysterious saying of His ?   This, I think—
All the old things of this world are to be made new
in the Kingdom of God, and all our old wines among
them.   When He Who sits upon the throne has
made all things new, there will be new heavens and
a new earth.   There will be a new Jerusalem, and
in the new Jerusalem a new upper room.   There
will be new vineyards, and new vines in that Holy
Land—our Heavenly Father all the time abiding
the Husbandman.

And then will be fulfilled the great promise
made of old to the evangelical prophet : " Now
will I sing to my well-beloved a song of my beloved
touching his vineyard.   My well-beloved hath a
vineyard in a very fruitful hill.   And I the Lord
do keep it : I will water it every moment : and
lest any hurt it, I will keep it night and day."

And then, when all the trees of Paradise restored shall say to that vine : " Come thou and reign over us " ; then shall that heavenly vine answer them and say : " How shall I leave my wine, which cheereth and maketh glad the heart of God and man, and go to be promoted over the other trees ? No ; I will not." And, then, concerning that new wine it will never be said : " Look not on it when it is red : when it giveth his colour in the cup " : for that heavenly wine will not bite like a serpent, and sting like an adder. But instead of that bitter proverb this sweet nuptial song shall be sung by the Bridegroom over the Bride : " I have come into my garden, my sister, my spouse : I have drunk my wine with my milk : eat, O friends : drink, yea, drink abundantly, O Beloved, of the running-over wine-cup of my everlasting love." Yes, communicants ! *So* shall it be said to you all ; and *so* shall it be done to you all, at the Marriage Supper of the Lamb.